More Praise for *The Great Workplace*

"A wonderful road map for becoming a great place to work. Burchell and Robin present a compelling case for improving workplace culture. This book is ideal for any leader who wishes to improve team effectiveness and make a difference in the organization. Inspiring!"

—Tim Felt, CEO, Colonial Pipeline

"Filled with practical examples of how great firms reinforce the trust, pride, and camaraderie essential to a great workplace. These are great ideas meant to be shared."

—Jim Weddle, managing partner, Edward Jones

"Well-researched and well-written, Burchell and Robin's book captures the essentials of what it takes to transition to a truly great workplace."

—Brian E. Keeley, president and CEO,
Baptist Health South Florida

"Many companies aim to be a great place to work, yet their leaders struggle with how to get there. Burchell and Robin do a wonderful job articulating the importance of building great workplace culture and provide great examples and ideas for how to achieve this. Everyone in a leadership position should read this book."

—Andrew Botwin, principal, Rothstein Kass

"Burchell and Robin tell real stories of how great organizations became (and remain) great workplaces by engaging the hearts and minds of the people who work there. The good news: the methods are transferable!"

—Peter J. Giammalvo, vice president, Organizational Development, OhioHealth

"*The Great Workplace* is a blueprint for all business owners who want to create and maintain a happy and productive workplace. A valuable guide for managers looking to empower their staff at every level."

—Jill Leonard Tavello, executive vice president of Culture, Stew Leonard's

the GREAT
WORKPLACE

the GREAT WORKPLACE

▼

HOW TO BUILD IT, HOW TO KEEP IT, AND
WHY IT MATTERS

MICHAEL BURCHELL

JENNIFER ROBIN

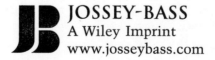

JOSSEY-BASS
A Wiley Imprint
www.josseybass.com

Published by Jossey-Bass
A Wiley Imprint
989 Market Street, San Francisco, CA 94103-1741—www.josseybass.com

Jossey-Bass books and products are available through most bookstores. To contact Jossey-Bass directly call our Customer Care Department within the U.S. at 800-956-7739, outside the U.S. at 317-572-3986, or fax 317-572-4002.

Jossey-Bass also publishes its books in a variety of electronic formats. Some content that appears in print may not be available in electronic books.

Library of Congress Cataloging-in-Publication Data
Burchell, Michael, 1967-
    The great workplace : how to build it, how to keep it, and why it matters / Michael Burchell, Jennifer Robin.
        p.   cm.
    Includes bibliographical references and index.
    ISBN 978-0-470-59626-5 (hardback), ISBN 978-0-470-93168-4 (ebk),
    ISBN 978-0-470-93171-4 (ebk), ISBN 978-0-470-93172-1 (ebk)
        1. Corporate culture.   2. Work environment.   3. Employee morale.   4. Organizational behavior.   5. Job satisfaction.   I. Robin, Jennifer, 1974-   II. Great Place to Work Institute.
    III. Title.
    HD58.7.B867   2011
    658.3'12—dc22

                                                                        2010034711

Printed in the United States of America
FIRST EDITION

HB Printing   10 9 8 7 6 5 4 3 2 1

This book is dedicated to employees at great workplaces all over the world. Their words and stories have shaped the model of a Great Place to Work® and forever changed how we think about workplaces.

CONTENTS

FOREWORD

By Robert Levering

Great Place to Work® Institute Cofounder

When I first picked up the manuscript of this book, I asked myself why I didn't write a similar book 20 years ago. *The Great Workplace: How to Build It, How to Keep It, and Why It Matters* gives practical advice to any leader who wants to transform his or her workplace culture. Indeed, it promises to help leaders achieve their organizational goals while having a positive impact on the working lives of their employees.

The reason I wondered why I hadn't tackled the same subject 20 years ago is that that was when I wrote *A Great Place to Work: What Makes Some Employers So Good—and Most So Bad* (Random House, 1988). In that book, I explained what distinguishes a great workplace from others based on what Milton Moskowitz and I observed in researching our best-selling 1984 book *The 100 Best Companies to Work for in America*. My definition of a great place to work became the basis for the Model that has been used by our Institute for its survey work and consulting, and is explained and discussed at length in this volume. So it would have been a logical next step for me, as a professional journalist and author of a half-dozen books on business subjects, to write the book that Michael

Burchell and Jennifer Robin have done so beautifully in the volume you're now holding in your hands.

As I read through Burchell and Robin's book, however, I understood that I was not the right person to have written this book. As experienced consultants, the two of them are in a much better position than I to offer practical advice to leaders. Prior to joining the Great Place to Work® Institute in 2003, Burchell had firsthand experience inside a great workplace as an HR leader at W. L. Gore & Associates, one of only four companies that have appeared on every FORTUNE 100 Best® list since 1998, as well as in our 1984 and 1993 books. At the Institute, Burchell has worked with dozens of companies all over the globe in applying the Great Place to Work® Model to a wide variety of business issues. A former board member of the Delaware chapter of the Society for Human Resource Management, he currently is involved with the Organization Development Network. Burchell received his doctorate in diversity and social justice from the University of Massachusetts Amherst.

Robin also spent three years in a consulting role at the Institute before writing this book, working with leaders of a wide spectrum of organizations in applying the Great Place to Work Model. Robin brings the added dimension of having taught human resource management for three years at Bradley University in undergraduate, master's, and executive programs. She has a particular passion for applying the cutting-edge policies and practices as seen in her previous book focused on work-life balance issues, *A Life in Balance: Finding Meaning in a Chaotic World* (coauthored with Charles Stoner, University Press of America, 2006). She received a doctorate in industrial organizational psychology from the University of Tennessee.

Besides their own personal experience as consultants and academics, the two authors conducted on-site interviews at thirteen great workplaces—Camden Property Trust, CH2M HILL, General Mills, Google, W. L. Gore & Associates, Hoar Construction, Holder Construction, Microsoft,

PricewaterhouseCoopers LLP, SAS, SC Johnson, Scripps Health, and
Wegmans Food Markets. At each of the firms, they interviewed the CEO
and top HR executives, and conducted a focus group with a group of
employees to fully understand their perspective. You will find studies
of these companies in *The Great Workplace* as well as extensive quotes
from their employees and leaders throughout the book.

Together, Burchell and Robin have produced a book that you
will find extremely useful, if for no other reason than it's chock full of
case studies as well as best practices from great workplaces, such as the
"responsibility statements" used at Edward Jones instead of job descriptions, or the "Vision Days" at Stew Leonards, or the "Back to Basics"
refresher course given to employees after five years working at J.M.
Smucker. While leaders may not be able to directly import any of these
best practices to their own organizations, they will undoubtedly find
themselves stimulated to emulate the kinds of practices used by their
peers at the best workplaces.

What makes this book especially significant is that Burchell and
Robin do a masterful job of explaining the "why" behind such practices.
They provide a framework for understanding why various practices help
to create a great workplace environment, which in turn helps an organization be more productive and foster more innovation.

Burchell and Robin's message is simple: any company can become
a great workplace, and this book can be your handbook to make yours
one of them.

PREFACE

This book was 25 years in the making.

The Great Place to Work Institute has recognized and studied great workplaces since the early 1980s, and today the Institute operates in over 40 countries and conducts the largest annual study of workplace environments globally. We publish lists of the best workplaces in each of these countries, and we also have published benchmark studies, white papers, research articles, and several books. We advise businesses, hold educational conferences, and conduct training programs on the lessons we have learned. And yet, leaders were always asking us when we were going to write "The Book"—a book that would illustrate in a practical way how leaders can take action to create a great workplace.

This book is an answer to those requests. In this book we endeavor to lay out the basic framework of what a great workplace is from an employee's perspective. While the voice of the employee takes center stage in this book, we have also incorporated the views and ideas of leaders, organizational best practices, and anecdotes and stories from our work as consultants. We have worked to draw upon the rich, deep experience that stems from studying great workplaces for over two decades. As you might imagine, we have learned a lot in that time, and we want to share with you a couple of things we now know.

We know and believe at our core that we can build a better society by helping companies transform their workplaces into great workplaces. Everyone benefits—individuals, organizations, families, and communities—when employees can give their best and know that the organization will also give them back its best. Yes, having a great workplace makes good business sense—as we will discover here—but at the end of the day, we believe that it is also the right thing to do.

We also know that great workplaces exist in every country, in every industry, and cut across organizations of all sizes and business models. Great workplaces exist in large, global organizations, small nonprofits, and government agencies as well. We believe your workplace can be a great workplace. This book aims to help you in that journey.

We know that the employee experience is central to understanding how to create a great workplace. It is the employee that determines whether his or her work environment is a great one, not the academic or business guru. As authors, we have had a front row in learning from these organizations—first and foremost by listening to their people. We have learned that great workplaces are at the same time simple and complex. We have tried to write this book in a rather straightforward, accessible style but still capture some of that complexity.

And finally, we know that leaders and organizations grow from the right amount of both challenge *and* support. This book aims to provide both. The challenge comes from the goal itself: to create and sustain a great workplace. Whether you cast that goal in language such as "be an employer of choice" or "have the best company to work for" or have a "fully engaged workforce" or win a "best company honor," the underlying challenge you have is to transform your workplace. The support comes from the words of employees, leaders, and the best practices from their companies. From our own experience, we can tell you that an understanding of what makes a great workplace deepens and becomes more nuanced over time. Eventually, it becomes second nature to consider your actions as a leader through the lens of the employee perspective. You will want to read this book and then keep it on hand to reference its best practices and stories. The final chapter gives suggestions on how to use best practices as you embark upon your own journey to a great workplace. We also encourage you to join our online community, which provides additional tips, tools, stories, and practices to support you along the way.

Both of us came to the Institute energized by the fact that it was our company that named hundreds of great workplaces around the world each year that we could learn from. Even more encouraging was that every year companies kept getting better. It energizes and encourages us now to know that your company may be the next list-maker. We wish you all the very best.

Michael and Jennifer
June 2010

the GREAT WORKPLACE

CHAPTER ONE

INTRODUCTION: THE VALUE OF CREATING GREAT WORKPLACES

*Ninety-five percent of my assets drive out the front gate every evening.
It's my job to bring them back.*
—JIM GOODNIGHT, CEO AND FOUNDER OF SAS

W hat makes a great workplace? It's not what you do. It's how
you do it.

If you are a leader, you must communicate, make decisions, and
interact with people, just as leaders in all companies do. You may carry
out your job description very well. But to be a leader in a great workplace,
you need to not only execute your role but also instill certain beliefs
in people as you are doing it. A great workplace is one where people
trust the people they work for, take pride in what they do, and enjoy
the people they work with. As a leader, you are the one to create and
reinforce these beliefs with every communication, every decision, every
interaction. To create a great workplace, you'll need to do your job
differently. It requires a mindshift; it requires viewing your employees
like Jim Goodnight suggests in the quote that opens this chapter. You'll
need to do your job realizing that how you do what you do makes a
world of difference to employees.

1

Consider the following quotes from employees in great workplaces:

"We have the culture where people are willing to talk to each other, share what they know, and take the proactive step to get you in touch with the right person."

"If you are a boss or a manager, you realize it's not about you. It's about empowering your people. And your voice doesn't carry any more weight than anyone else's. The only way this [management style] will work is by nurturing and nudging and helping set some vision."

"Our company has growing pains like any company, but the people always come first. I truly know that I matter in this corporation, and that's what keeps me here."

What do people say about your company, division, or workgroup? Do they say it's a great place to work? If you don't yet have a great workplace, it can be. And if it is already a great workplace, you can hang on to it. This book will show you how. Not by handing over a list of initiatives or steps, but by orienting you to a different way of doing things. We won't tell you what to do, but we will tell you how to do it.

THE KNOWLEDGE BASE

The content of this book is based on years of research. Our company, the Great Place to Work Institute, has been studying great workplaces since its inception in 1991. But research began much earlier, in the early 1980s, when cofounder Robert Levering and Milton Moskowitz were approached by Addison-Wesley Publishing to write a book on the best places to work in America. When Robert and Milton set out to interview people in companies around the country in 1980, business outcomes were not a key consideration. Rather, Robert and Milton believed that treating people well was the right thing to do, and so they focused exclusively on the employee experience. Still, they expected to see a connection between the companies with the happiest employees and the companies with the healthiest bottom lines. They also anticipated that they would see consistent practices among the best workplaces, those that Robert and Milton deemed the 100 best in America. From those consistencies, they hoped they could discern a recipe for creating a great workplace that could be followed by any leader in any organization.

In their 1984 book, *The 100 Best Companies to Work for in America*, Levering and Moskowitz described the experience of employees at the 100 best workplaces among the hundreds they researched. The *New York Times* bestseller provided informative stories about all 100 companies, and highlighted several aspects they shared, including opportunities, pay and benefits, and openness. Themes began to emerge about the characteristics of great workplaces, but what made great workplaces that way weren't categories of practices or policies.

Turns out that the intuitively obvious prediction, that organizations with the most creative practices and the best bottom lines would be the ones employees raved about, was not universally true. Something was going on that transcended the policies and practices at the best companies to work for. It wasn't *what* they were doing, it was *how* their leaders were doing it. Specifically, the practices companies had and the money leaders spent on employees did not always lead to great workplaces; the relationships they built in the process did.

In Levering's 1988 book, *A Great Place to Work: What Makes Some Employers So Good—And Most So Bad*, he discussed great workplaces in terms of relationships and put forth the definition of a Great Place to Work that opened this chapter and that appears throughout this book.

Specifically, he identified the relationships between employees and their leaders, between employees and their jobs, and between employees and each other as the indicators of a great place to work. Relationships at work matter, and in particular, the centrality of these three relationships influenced people's loyalty, commitment, and willingness to contribute to organizational goals and priorities. If leaders implemented practices and created programs and policies that contributed to these three relationships, employees had a great workplace experience. It mattered less what the programs, policies, and practices were, and more that they were done in a way that strengthened relationships. The Great Place to Work Model (see Figure 1.1) was developed during this time by the Institute's founders, Robert Levering and Amy Lyman. The Model was later formalized and today has five dimensions, which form the core chapters of this book: Credibility, Respect, Fairness (which, put together, comprise Trust); Pride; and Camaraderie.

Figure 1.1   The Great Place to Work Model

In the late 1990s, FORTUNE magazine approached the Institute to develop an annual list of the best companies to work for in America. Now the FORTUNE 100 Best Companies to Work For® list is released every January in one of the magazine's best-selling issues. While the FORTUNE list tends to showcase the perks and benefits that employees in those companies enjoy, those perks are not the reason the companies made the list in the first place. They made the list because of their leaders' ability to create strong relationships. They made the list because of the five dimensions.

Not only have these five hallmarks stood the test of time, they are also applicable to companies regardless of size or geographic location. The idea of great workplaces and the practical Model quickly spread beyond the United States. Now, in over 40 countries around the world, the Great Place to Work Institute has shown that organizations and their employees thrive when these hallmarks are woven into actions on the part of their leaders.

All told, the Institute surveys 2 million people and gathers data on the cultures of nearly 6,000 companies worldwide every year. We evaluate companies for list membership using consistent methodology, whether the company is 60 people or 6,000, located in Brazil or India. In these evaluations, we assess two aspects of workplaces. The first aspect, weighted more heavily, is the employee experience. The Institute administers a survey called the Trust Index© to determine the consistency of trust, pride, and camaraderie in the workplace and to learn directly from employees what makes their workplace great.

The second aspect we evaluate for our best companies lists are the programs, policies, and practices leaders put in place for their employees. Using our Culture Audit©, trained evaluators assess each organization, and care is taken to calibrate ratings across the hundreds of companies that apply each year. From the Culture Audits, the Institute gathers thousands of best practices that, like the survey's employee comments, breathe life into the concepts of trust, pride, and camaraderie. These practices range from Boston Consulting Group's policy of giving seasoned veterans incentives to have lunch with new hires, to ACUITY's Gossip Lines, wherein CEO Ben Salzmann shares information and personal stories via blast voicemail.

The Institute holds several annual conferences around the world that bring leaders from the recognized organizations together to share their stories, and we maintain close ties with the list-makers, learning from them through site visits, interviews, and focus groups. As team members with the Institute, the two of us have at our fingertips scores of best practices and employee comments that help us help leaders build stronger relationships with their people. We use this wealth of information in our role as consultants, wherein we're hired by companies who want to improve the relationships in their organizations.

Over time, we've learned a thing or two about creating great workplaces, and this book is about sharing what we've learned with you. You'll find many examples of best practices from the best companies, practices that build the relationships of trust, pride, and camaraderie. Many of these practices were submitted by the companies themselves as part of their consideration for the list. In other cases, we've talked to employees and leaders specifically for this book; we asked them what they want you to know about creating and sustaining a great workplace. What is still astounding to us, after years working closely with the best, is that there is no end to the ways you can build relationships through your practices. Your practices will look different than many of those mentioned in this book, but as you create your great workplace, keep in mind three fundamental relationships.

THE THREE RELATIONSHIPS

People have a choice every day in how they mentally approach their work. Though most of us ultimately work for some blend of financial goals and personal fulfillment, we each choose how we *think* about our work. People can consider work a necessity or a blessing, a burden or an opportunity. While the choice is not as simplistic as that, putting it in stark terms does help you think more critically about how the decisions you make as a leader influence how your employees see their work.

We began asking people about how their workplace shaped their approach to work in 1980, when Levering and Moskowitz asked thousands of employees, "Is your organization a great place to work?" and "Why?" While the context in which people respond has changed quite a bit since then, their answers point to strikingly consistent experiences. Specifically, they believe their leaders to be credible, respectful, and fair—they trust them. They also take pride in what they do, and they share a sense of camaraderie with their coworkers. Without trust, pride, and camaraderie, any measure of business success is diminished.

Therein lies an important insight. Because the relationships you create matter, *you* are the critical difference between a very good company and a very great company. In the best companies, leaders at all levels have a strong commitment to creating strong ties between the employee and the organization. Indeed, enhancing trust, pride, and camaraderie in the workplace is *the* central task of effective leadership in today's organization.

Trust

It is often said that employees tend to join organizations, but leave their managers. While not a universal truth, it is often the case that employees look for new opportunities when they determine they have irreconcilable relationships with their supervisors. On the other hand, when an employee says and genuinely means, "I trust the people I work for," leaders, the employee, and the organization all benefit. Not only is the risk of turnover lessened, but the workflow is easier and more gratifying.

If you step back from your workplace and consider for a moment the people in your life whom you really trust and who trust you, you know that agreeing upon goals, communicating needs and issues, and relying upon them to follow through is easier and quicker. People in trusting relationships sometimes develop a shorthand way of communicating that helps to speed up information flow. Further, when a difficult issue comes up, the individuals in the relationship seek to preserve the relationship and give one another the benefit of the doubt. A similar pattern appears in trusting business relationships—we are not always second-guessing motives, and we can rely on other people to follow through on their commitments.

Trust also supports enhanced cooperation. When we trust one another in our teams, we are more likely to encourage mutual growth, seek the win-win, and resolve conflicts more constructively. We are more willing to give extra to get the job done. In all of these ways, the trust that a manager helps to foster with his or her team matters. Trust is the primary relationship.

This is evidenced by the nuanced way that employees we surveyed talked about trusting their leaders. Employees described three qualities that are necessary to their experience of trust, and these three qualities are the first three dimensions of the Great Place to Work Model. The first, Credibility, involves the sense that leaders give employees appropriate information, are competent to lead the organization, and that their actions match their words. The second, Respect, refers to the employees' beliefs that leaders support them personally and professionally, that they wish to collaborate with them on suggestions and decisions, and that leaders care about them as people and not just as employees. The final group of perceptions, Fairness, involves the belief that leaders create a level playing field, treating people equitably and impartially, and allowing them to voice concerns about decisions.

An example that speaks to all three qualities can be found in a story about Plante & Moran, a Michigan-based accounting firm and a list-maker since 1999. They proclaim that the company is "relatively jerk-free" right in the philosophy statement. The story behind the claim is that founding partner Frank Moran once told a fellow staff member that Plante & Moran doesn't hire jerks, hence leaving the organization jerk-free. But the staff member replied that we are all jerks at times. Frank conceded this point and settled for the statement that the company is "relatively jerk-free." In this simple statement, Plante & Moran communicates its goal to hire the best people (Credibility), its nurturing and understanding work environment (Respect), and its commitment to holding everyone to a similar standard (Fairness). All leaders set expectations for people, but Plante & Moran builds credibility, respect, and fairness in their approach. Each of these anchors of trust will be discussed later in the book.

Pride

The second of the three relationships found in great workplaces (and the fourth dimension of the Great Place to Work Model) is the relationship between the individual and his or her work. Essentially, people experience a great workplace when they feel as though they make a difference in their organization, that their work is meaningful. They are also proud of their team's accomplishments, and the contributions the organization makes to the community at large. Often, pride comes from the employee's sense that he or she contributes to the organization's values, the goods and services it produces, and the philanthropic contributions the organization makes to better their communities. While largely internalized, a healthy sense of pride can be bolstered by actions on the part of the organization.

Many of these actions will be discussed in the chapter on Pride, but for now, consider Recreation Equipment Inc. (REI). While best known as a nationwide retailer of quality outdoor gear and apparel, REI's employees know they are contributing to a higher goal. REI is committed to getting people active outdoors, increasing access to outdoor recreation, and reducing its own impact on the environment. Pictures of employees participating in outdoor activities are posted on the walls of every store, and employees are routinely involved in community outreach projects. While REI might attract individuals who already have an affinity for the outdoors, the opportunities REI offers employees capitalizes upon and multiplies this sense of pride.

Camaraderie

Great workplaces foster healthy and strong relationships between people, and given this, the final dimension of the Great Place to Work Model is Camaraderie. At great workplaces, people feel welcomed from the very first day, through everything from formal orientation activities to meaning-ful interactions with coworkers and mentors. They feel as though every-one is working toward one common goal, and that they can be authentic at work. While some degree of camaraderie can be attributed to good hiring, organizations also take action to build a sense of family at work. They provide opportunities for employees to collaborate and interact out-side of work. Some also provide outlets for employees to help one another in times of need. Still others celebrate the unique gifts of their employees that may not otherwise be discovered in the course of a normal workday.

Starbucks, a global purveyor of tea and coffee, is a company that encourages camaraderie. In each of its 15,000 stores, partners (Starbucks' term for "employees") get to know each other better by sharing free beverages a half-hour before and after their shift. This allows partners to interact with one another off-the-clock, but enjoying a cup of coffee or tea on the company.

These five dimensions—and three relationships they fall under—will provide a vocabulary with which you might better understand great workplaces, a lens through which you can consider the health of the relationships in your organization, and a framework for you to make systematic changes to your workplace. A summary of the Model is presented in Figure 1.1.

THE ATTITUDE ADJUSTMENT

Lest you think trust, pride, and camaraderie are "nice to haves" rather than essentials, consider the stories of two leaders, Tony Parella and Chris Van Gorder.

Tony Parella is the CEO of Shared Technologies, a company that installs and maintains high-end telecommunications equipment. The company has been owned by WorldCom, Intermedia, and Allegiance Telecom, all of which went into bankruptcy. The staff was demoralized by the financial and operational challenges, and trust in the workplace was low. Parella believed there had to be a better way, and he and his management team undertook the difficult task of rebuilding trust. In four short years, Parella took the organization from Chapter 11 bankruptcy to a 45 percent compounded annual growth rate. As he put it in a talk given at the 2009 Great Place to Work Institute Conference, "In 2005, Shared Technologies' employee survey results returned an average approval rating of 59 percent. In 2007, the exact same survey resulted in an overall approval rating of 96 percent. That's a 37 percent improvement. Shared Technologies has grown by 45 percent, year after year, while the rest of our industry has had, at best, single-digit growth. . . . When employees feel good about their work life and their company, they deliver above-market results for investors" (Parella, 2008, p. 73–74).

Chris Van Gorder is the CEO of Scripps Health, which faced a series of organizational challenges back in 2001. Scripps was incurring significant operating losses, had acquired a health unit that also was incurring monthly losses, and was experiencing sizable financial impact from their efforts to comply with new California legislation. Added to this was high turnover among staff, broken communication channels, and labor shortages. Scripps' internal employee survey also indicated variable levels of trust in management. Through a concerted effort to focus on the organization's strategic objectives, which included work-force development and trust-building measures, Scripps increased profitability by $62 million in four years. Moreover, turnover, vacancy rates in hard-to-fill positions, workers' compensation claims, and health care costs all decreased, and employee survey results soared.

As Van Gorder puts it, "We never want to get cocky, and we know that things will come along that are going to put a real strain on us. But if we put enough credibility in the bank and take care of our people, our people are going to take us through it. If we don't, we will fail. And that is what being a great place to work is all about. And that is the return on investment. It is not immediate, necessarily. And I don't know how tangible it is. I don't think you could come up with dollars and cents, but when I was recently with all the top hospital systems in the state, and they were going around talking about all their woes, I was a little embar-rassed. We are not having those challenges. And we are in the toughest marketplace in California."

Shared Technologies and Scripps Health are not unique. Indeed, in research done on the best companies to work for, we see consistent evidence of their financial success. Russell Investment Group conducts an annual assessment of the financial performance of the publicly traded 100 Best against the S&P 500 and the Russell 3000. For example, from 1998–2008, the 100 Best achieved annualized stock returns of 6.8 percent, with the S&P 500 coming in at 1.04 percent and the Russell 3000 at 1.25 percent. Table 1.1 highlights this trend over time. Related studies of the financial performance of the best companies in other countries such as Denmark, the U.K., and Brazil also confirm this trend.

Table 1.1

The work of Alex Edmans at the Wharton School provides further evidence. In his 2007 study, Edmans analyzed the relationship between employee satisfaction and long-run stock performance. He utilized the FORTUNE 100 Best Companies to Work For list over an eight-year period, and even when controlling for other factors (such as risk or industry), found that the 100 Best portfolio earned over double the market returns by the end of 2005. High-trust workplaces consistently outperform lower-trust workplaces (Edmans, 2010).

Other comparisons between the list-makers and the rest indicate more immediate financial implications of trust. For instance, we know that the best places to work have lower turnover as compared to the statistics compiled by the Bureau of Labor Statistics, more job applicants as compared to applicants to the list that do not achieve recognition, and in the U.K., lower absenteeism than companies not recognized for their workplace cultures.

As Jim Goodnight, Founder and CEO of SAS, an analytic software company, notes, "It turns out that doing the right thing, treating people right, is also the right thing for the company." Indeed it is. SAS generally has about 4 percent turnover every year, in an industry that tends to average around 20 percent. Estimates by Professor Jeffrey Pfeffer of Stanford University indicate that the company saves between $75–100 million annually—a figure that drops right to the bottom line. Further, stable project teams support overall efficiency, quality, and long-term customer relationships. (Additional information on the return on investment and related studies can be found at this book's website, www .thegreatworkplaceonline.com.)

What's driving these results? Sometimes it is the *lack* of unnecessary disruptions and stress (like those found in a low-trust environment) that lead to positive financial success. When people mistrust their leaders, feel stuck in a meaningless job, or feel as though they don't know their coworkers well enough to be themselves, they tend to ruminate and lose focus. Not to mention, people don't usually bound out of bed to arrive in such an environment, nor do they stay much past the formal end of their workday to finish up a project important to the company's growth and success.

In order to understand the financial implications of this state of mind, consider for a moment the cost to a business if a product ships late, or a piece of equipment breaks down, or a critical system crashes. These costs can usually be calculated to the dollar, and they often are. We even have terms for these problems, such as "system down time." Consider, however, the costs to a business if two employees get into an unproductive exchange, and then return to their work stations or offices. They aren't focused on the task at hand; instead, they are still thinking about the frustrating interaction they just had with their colleague. Or consider the implication if a team leader fails to address unclear roles or goals. The team lurches along, marginally productive but wholly ineffective.

Very smart leaders can often calculate the cost of one defective product, or one lost customer. But what would be the cost of all of the lost time that is built in to unhealthy relationships at work?

Terri Kelly is the CEO of W. L. Gore & Associates, an innovative company that researches, develops, and manufactures fluoropolymer-based products, the most well known being Gore-Tex® fabric. She suggests that most companies have seen an underperforming team in action. When a team underperforms, she says, "You're spending hours on end in meetings because there's no trust, there's no relationship, there's no desire to work together, and people hunker down. I can't even think about the productivity drain when you've got that kind of environment." That's why Gore invests early to make sure teams are high performing. "You've got to have them build relationships. They have to invest the time to get to know each other, not just their technical abilities, but what they're all about and what perspective they can bring," Kelly says. "We see this as an investment in furthering our teams so they are really high-performing teams. They have a totally different level of ownership and responsibility for the company. We have not gone to the precision of trying to measure that financially, but there is no doubt that there is a strong linkage that goes directly back to our strategic intent."

Data can prove to you how high-trust relationships yield tangible business benefits and unhealthy relationships result in disengaged employees, people down time, and other hard or soft costs. However, as a leader, even if you are a believer, that isn't enough. You will need to put your beliefs into action, and no amount of data or statistics can do the work for you. Wegmans Food Markets is a grocery store chain based in Rochester, New York. CEO Danny Wegman suggests, "Things get in the way of letting people be human. Particularly quarterly reports and business schools. I think what we try to do is make it very clear that what's important is doing the right thing. And if we do the right thing, all the other things take care of themselves."

One hurdle, then, is learning to trust that there are bottom line results when leaders do the right thing. There are other hurdles as well, shifts you'll need to make in your own thinking in order to fully embrace the idea of a great workplace. While the best places to work and the people who lead them are nothing short of phenomenal, they are not a product of magic or luck. Good workplaces become great when leaders just like you deliberately and reliably focus upon building trust, pride, and camaraderie with people in the organization. Other hurdles that may be stopping you are predictable: time; the "if it ain't broke, don't fix it" mentality; and tunnel vision.

Who Has the Time?
In a rapidly changing environment, we react to what is in front of us. There are big issues to deal with: competition, globalization, legislation, and natural disasters. And there are the more mundane, but often more pressing issues like turnover, budget shortfalls, and deliverables.

Trust grows from how the leader reacts to these changes—it's a by-product, if you will. If a leader reacts adeptly, while considering the needs of employees and maintaining a level playing field for all, trust is strengthened. But rarely are you attending to the relational consequences of your every move. This is not because you don't understand the importance of relationships, but because you need to put out the next fire. This is admirable. A leader is rarely successful if he or she can't move nimbly through the changing environment.

But what leaders often miss is that their ability to mobilize others to meet these challenges alongside them depends upon how much leaders are trusted. If people don't trust their leaders, they hesitate, weigh the consequences of action and inaction, and may determine that the safest thing to do is wait and see. For example, do you want your employees to spend their time and energy on a marketing opportunity that you are sure will increase sales? If they don't trust you, you'll have a hard time getting them to do so without painstakingly convincing them or resorting to unpleasant ultimatums. And, in the time it takes you to get them on board, you may lose the opportunity. On the other hand, if they trust you, employees have confidence in the direction you set and put forth effort readily. Even if your hunch isn't right about the opportunity, they'll give you the latitude to make mistakes along the way.

Whatever tangible issue you are dealing with will probably change again, but trust with employees underlies everything. The upshot is this: while time may prevent you from thinking systematically about your workplace relationships, the shortage of time is one reason you are wise to think systematically about your workplace relationships. Things move along more smoothly when relationships are strong, and when time is short, this can be the difference between success and failure.

I Really Don't Think Trust Is My Problem. If It Ain't Broke, Don't Fix It

Sheer statistics tell you otherwise. In the most recent Edelman Trust Barometer (2010)—a global survey of people in 22 countries on 5 continents that investigates the trust afforded to leaders, institutions, and businesses—it was determined that people trust information from peers, industry analysts, and academics more than they trust information coming from a CEO. Less than 30 percent of people surveyed in the U.S. believe information from a CEO is credible.

The tricky thing about trust is that there are no obvious and early indicators for a low-trust environment. If there are problems with a piece of equipment, defect rates rise or output decreases. If there are problems with investments, returns fall. If there is a problem with marketing or sales, market share drops. For many business problems, there is (quantifiable) smoke before there is fire.

This is not the case with trust. Without trust, business can carry on, but whatever outcomes are being achieved are not the best a company can do. That is to say, without trust, people still come to work, still carry out their assigned tasks, still pass their work on to the next person. Though the contributions they make are not nearly what they'd be capable of in an environment of trust, they may be producing enough that you don't even know you have a problem. As trust diminishes in an organization, or even if it was never built in the first place, it may take time before leaders realize they've lost it. Like with all relationships, trust is often difficult to build, especially after it has been breached. It is much easier to nurture the trust you have already earned than to build it from scratch.

On the other hand, in environments where trust is present and nurtured, people show up for *years*. Turnover is lower, which increases efficiency and reduces recruiting and hiring costs. In high-trust environments, people not only do their work, they constantly work to improve their work, and they take calculated risks that benefit the organization. In high-trust environments, people know each other well; they work together to accomplish greater outcomes while building strong relationships that maximize development and create a sense of belonging.

Once again, the reason you are not focused on relationships is exactly why you should be. You may not be focused on relationships because you are not seeing any signs they are breaking down, but those signs won't show up until the business suffers. Attend to it now, before it's too late.

Shouldn't I Be Focusing on the Business Instead?

Yes . . . and no. Yes, you should be focusing on the business. No, you should not do that *instead* of focusing on relationships. And quite simply, you can't just focus on the business, even if you want to. The way you make every business decision (the *how*, not the *what*) affects your relationships with people, like it or not. The sum total of the three relationships we've been talking about can be thought of as the culture of your organization, and you help create that culture with every acquisition you oversee, employee you hire, and problem you resolve.

It's true that a lot of the time, the business problems companies face are largely unrelated to the "people" side of the business. Still, the resolution of the problems contributes to culture. For instance, at Gore, leaders recognized early on that they would need to keep an entrepreneurial spirit in order to be successful in the marketplace. While they could have solved this problem any number of ways, Gore chose to do so by providing employees with as much flexibility as possible. People are hired for a role, but they choose the projects they wish to work on. Associates are held accountable for their commitments to projects, and Gore reaps the benefits of the increased energy, creativity, and entrepreneurship that come with personal choice. The business problem of sustained entrepreneurial spirit was solved by respecting the needs of employees and thereby building trust.

Companies also face problems that *are* clearly related to the people side of things, problems like employee attraction, retention, engagement, and performance. Many tech companies, including Microsoft and SAS, realize that the talent pipeline for their industry starts with grades K–12. Both have programs to engage and inspire this group, and perhaps to plant the seed for eventual employees! Microsoft hosts DigiGirlz days and summer camps each year to educate high school junior girls about careers in technology, and to break down some of the stereotypes of the industry. Cofounders of SAS started a secondary school, Cary Academy, to integrate technology into the learning process. While each company could have addressed this people problem differently, they each have married its solution with their values and passions to create an even stronger organizational culture.

Regardless of whether it is a business problem or a people problem, culture is a by-product of resolving it successfully. When equipment breaks down and a capital investment is required, trust is built when you involve employees in the decision, train them appropriately, and thank them for their help in making the transition a success. When cost cuts are required, trust is built when you engage people in finding places to save money, share the burden with employees, and use layoffs as a last resort.

On the flip side, you will gain little traction if you set out to create culture by generating a set of initiatives or projects that exist separately from your company's operational challenges and opportunities. When leaders champion cultural changes that do not solve real business problems, or that exist in a vacuum apart from the company's operating environment, they fail. They become the dreaded "flavor of the month" that employees learn to dismiss as soon as the fanfare from the launch wears off. So, it is less important that you create new initiatives, and more important that you change the way you are executing on the things that help make your organization successful. So yes, focus on the business.

The assumption that the relationships of trust, pride, and camaraderie do not hold a candle to the priority of time-pressed, financial, and operating investments is a faulty one. While we don't argue about the wisdom of focusing time, energy, and resources on the business, we submit that it is a false choice to place attention here rather than on the culture. The resolution of such issues *becomes* the culture, and no amount of compartmentalization into business issues and people issues can change that. The business issues are the people issues, and the people issues are the business issues.

Though we've just addressed three common and predictable hurdles, there are doubtless many more. Attitudes build up over a long period of time, and it is no small thing to change them. But the benefits of doing so are countless. If people trust the people they work for, they are willing to take more risks, follow in times of uncertainty, and assume the best intentions on the part of leaders. If people have pride in what they do, the quality of their work matters personally, and they'll talk about their experiences with neighbors and friends, which in turn improves the reputation of the organization. If people like their cowork-ers, they are happy to help out in times of need, and to welcome new employees in ways that exceed their expectations and bind them to the company from day one. First and foremost, adjust your attitude. See relationships as important aspects of your business success. Imbue your actions with trust, pride, and camaraderie.

BEGINNING THE JOURNEY

As you begin, know that it starts with you; *you* are the person to make these changes in your organization. Change is not a program, an initiative, or a policy. "We try to be very careful about talking about initiatives and programs. You can easily wind up in a position of initiative overload," says Michael Fenlon, a Human Capital Leader at PricewaterhouseCoo-pers LLP, a professional service firm. He goes on, "Also, sometimes when we talk about a program or initiative, it is something . . . that is part of the culture, the fabric, the DNA of the place." Fenlon talks about employee development as an example of a cultural element that does not rely solely upon a formalized program. Rather, employee develop-ment comes from the behavior of each and every leader. "So much of high performance is about setting high expectations *and* creating a feedback-rich environment, recognizing and celebrating accomplish-ments, instilling a sense of purpose and meaning, and investing in development. We emphasize coaching within the engagement team, offering feedback in real time and in the moment. So while we invest in formal development programs that also foster networking and a sense of community, our fundamental approach is integrating development within our engagements and as part of achieving sustained high performance within our teams."

We often joke that our jobs as consultants would be so much easier if we could help leaders roll out a "Trust Policy." Essentially, it would decree that from this day forward, everyone will trust everyone else. In some ways, building trust is easier than generating a policy; all it requires you to do is to behave differently. In other ways, though, building trust is infinitely more difficult. It requires you to consider the impacts of your decisions on relationships, to craft and support organizational policies and procedures that position your managers to do the same, and to build a self-sustaining system of trust with employees.

Moreover, no two great workplaces look the same, and the only way you will determine what is best for your company is to engage in practices that will give you feedback as to what works. While the rest of this book gives examples, insights, and best practices for creating strong relationships, you are the only one who can determine what it looks like in your organization. We give suggestions for how to go about this in Chapter 8.

The important point, though, is to begin the journey by doing things differently. We agree with several leaders who have pointed out that it is easier to act your way into a new way of thinking than it is to think your way into a new way of acting. But while it is important to get started, it is also important to remember that the journey takes time. If you and your leadership team have not been factoring in relationships as a key aspect of your decision making, it might seem a daunting task to begin to do that now. Some leaders are most successful when they start small. Perhaps they shift weekly meetings that are mostly one-way communication to working meetings where everyone puts their heads together to solve a pressing problem. We worked with one leader who shifted his one-on-one meetings with his staff from his office to theirs, demonstrating respect for their time and signaling that he valued each as a person. Another leader began blasting voicemails that included both business and personal items in order to increase his accessibility. Over time, what leaders learn in these small changes lays the groundwork for a cultural shift that includes changes in organizational policies, leadership development, and operating procedures. You'll read about some of those changes, and more, in the chapters to come.

In the next few chapters, we will discuss the *behaviors* associated with building relationships at work. And we ground these behaviors in the employee's experience. We made this pair of choices deliberately. The first, because many times leaders get stuck when starting out, and behaviors are the only thing in your control. And the second, because by focusing on the outcome—the employee experience—you will be able to see how to put these concepts into practice. But changing behavior is not an end in and of itself; it is a catalyst for a larger process whereby attitudes and relationships change. And, ultimately, so does the organizational culture.

SAS: TAKING CARE OF THEIR GREATEST ASSET

Fast Facts:

- Software developer
- Based in Cary, NC
- Founded in 1976
- Privately held
- 5,566 employees in the United States; 11,055 in offices around the world
- List-maker since 1998, with recognition in the 1993 book; recognized internationally forty-eight times

SAS is widely recognized as a great workplace. In fact, SAS is often cited as an inspiration by many of today's list-makers for their own facilities, wellness programs, and benefits. Even today, more than 34 years since its founding, SAS's list of benefits for employees is jaw-dropping. Some of the most unique include

- An on-site Health Care Center with a 56-member staff. There is no cost to employees or their covered dependents. A SAS pediatric health care provider is available by phone during the evening, weekend, and holiday hours for breastfeeding mothers and parents of young infants with questions and concerns.
- An on-site childcare facility at headquarters for over 600 children, affiliated with the American Montessori Society. All full-time employees with one year of service are eligible to apply for placement, and when there is a waiting list, acceptance is based on length of time with the company, not on an employee's position in the organization. Parents at regional offices receive a childcare subsidy that is comparable to the on-site benefit.
- Eldercare resources such as supportive networking opportunities; consultants; professional guidance for advance care directives; and a Caring Closet stocked with wheelchairs, crutches, shower seats, and more.

- A 66,000-square-foot recreation and fitness facility with a class schedule similar to those found at community gyms. SAS goes the extra mile, though, and also offers specialty classes such as an intramural swim league, a modern dance class, and an indoor rowing crew.
- Wellness and health classes and programs such as an Eco-family Challenge (where families record and earn points for earth-friendly activities), Tween/Teen Culinary Camp, sailing lessons, skateboard instruction, daddy-daughter dances, spring gardening workshops, and more.

Significantly, SAS doesn't set out to be the best when it comes to benefits. They set out to be the most creative and innovative software developer around. Jennifer Mann, Vice President of Human Resources, puts it this way: "Creativity is especially important to SAS because software is a product of the mind. Creativity doesn't come on demand. We're all inspired at different times. At SAS, we create a stimulating and flexible work environment, which allows employees to work when they are most innovative and productive. We trust them to do their jobs. From day one, SAS has taken a very organic approach to developing its benefits and programs. We focus on the employee. Benefits happen when there is a need, not because we have a task force or special initiative." Dr. Jim Goodnight, founder of SAS and a software developer himself, is said to have wanted to create a place he would like to come to work every day.

His vision for a great workplace resonates with employees. SAS enjoys a 4 percent turnover rate, as compared to a 20 percent turnover rate in its industry. Employees appreciate the longevity of their coworkers. One says, "I'm a lawyer here, and my job is to protect our intellectual property. I can go get patent registrations, trademark registrations, copyright registrations, but I can't protect what's in our good people's heads. The payback to the company for having a great culture is that we keep good people. They're not hopping

Case Study

from job to job carrying the things they've invented. Plus, we're not always having to retrain people. All of this makes our lives a whole lot easier." Another employee says, "That longevity translates into really strong relationships with our customers in terms of sales, consultation, and tech support. There's this deep-rooted ownership in terms of how the company does as a whole."

Most important, though, employees feel cared for as people. In talking about his delight with the childcare leave that his leader at SAS encouraged him to take, one employee said, "I'll never forget that. It's such a difference from the 'Why did you take a day off?!' that I received at a previous employer. At SAS, leaders seem to understand that I'm going to be here a long time. I've been here ten years, what's two weeks? It seems like a small thing, but for me it was huge."

Dr. Goodnight's overarching philosophy is that "if you treat employees as if they make a difference to the company, they will make a difference to the company." The facilities, benefits, and perks send the message that employees make a difference. At SAS, employees keep coming back.

CHAPTER TWO

CREDIBILITY
"I believe in my leaders."

*I think the most fun part of my job is getting out and talking to associates. We have a
number of forums. It's a great high for me because I can come in and talk to
100 or 200 associates at once and share my views, but more importantly,
they can share their perspective. It's music to my ears, how excited they
are to be working on their projects and watching the culture in action.
It's very motivating because [culture is] not just a theory;
you see it in practice.*

—TERRI KELLY, CEO AT W. L. GORE & ASSOCIATES

*I can sit in a room with Terri Kelly and really battle out a difference of opinion and feel
no fear of repercussion as a result of that kind of behavior. In fact, it's the expected
behavior. We have the opportunity to connect wherever we need to connect to
take on whatever might be the issue or the opportunity of the day.*

—EMPLOYEE AT W. L. GORE & ASSOCIATES

We wrote a lot in the last chapter about the crucial focus on trust in the employee-leader relationship. Credibility is the first major building block of a trusting relationship, and therefore we want to narrow our focus and explore what it means in depth. As the above quotes illustrate, Credibility is a two-way street. But it is you, the leader, who initiates the relationship.

If you've read anything about leadership in the last ten years, you've read about credibility. Often mentioned as a foundational characteristic of effective leadership in the popular press, it refers to a leader's trustworthiness, expertise, and authenticity. Leaders gain credibility by setting the course, supporting employees, and helping the organization to reach its goals while being approachable and honest.

When we look at a leader's credibility through the Great Place to Work lens, we look at three things: the degree to which leaders share information with people (two-way communication), the ability to display expertise while remaining open and accessible to employees (competence), and the extent to which the leaders' actions match their words (integrity).

When you've built credibility, you can spend more time on the things that matter. When you have set the organization's direction, made expectations clear, and communicated thoroughly, you spend less time watching over people's shoulders or correcting errors. Moreover, people can make decisions without checking their approach, even if they've never run across the specific situation they are facing. Take employees at Nordstrom, a fashion specialty store with locations across the U.S. They have boiled their expectations down to one sentence: "Use good judgment in all situations." They show employees what that looks like by consistently communicating and role modeling behavior. One VP at Nordstrom explains, "I know that the people who run the company are going to work as hard—or harder— than me. The same principles that were here before I got here will be in place after I retire. That's encouraging. I really like that. You can't teach a culture. You have to live it. You have to experience it. You have to share it. You have to show it."

Imagine if each and every one of your employees treated their work like it was part of their own business. That's what Nordstrom leaders enjoy. And that's what allows them the time and energy to do their jobs as leaders—anticipating trends and improving sales—rather than monitoring every move of their employees.

When you've gained credibility, people follow your lead because they believe in you, because they know you will lead them and the organization to success. As you'll see throughout Chapter 2, credibility saves you time and increases productivity. Above all, acting credibly makes you a leader. Sure, there are other, seemingly faster ways to get employees to comply. Through the force of your authority and your ability to reward and punish them, they will fulfill their duties. But it is the relationship you build with your people that gets you the commitment needed not merely to fulfill daily duties but to go above and beyond.

TWO-WAY COMMUNICATION

Two-way communication, competence, and integrity are all critical to Credibility, but communication is particularly important. Communication influences not just the employee's perception of your credibility but his or her entire *experience* of the workplace. In fact, when we are working with organizations, we often recommend shoring up communication before tackling anything else. Why? When we talk with employees about their experiences at great workplaces, they routinely emphasize their appreciation for communication. When they're not talking explicitly about the importance of communication, they're discussing aspects of their work environment that rest upon healthy communication between leaders and employees. Once genuine two-way communication exists, it can be used as a vehicle to support others, collaborate with them, and signal caring (relevant in Chapter 3, "Respect"). Furthermore, when people have the information they need to understand business decisions, even if the decisions don't always work out in their favor, they are more likely to report a level playing field (a hallmark of Chapter 4, "Fairness"). If you were to work on one single aspect of a great workplace, you'd likely make far-reaching improvements by strengthening two-way communication.

Employees talk about two main aspects of communication when we ask them what makes their workplace great. In the first place, they talk about *informative* communication. This occurs when leaders give them the information they need to do their jobs and make expectations clear. You might think of it as the group of communications that travel from leaders to employees. Frankly, when most leaders think of communication, they think of this half of the equation. But informative communication isn't the whole story. Employees also discuss *accessible* communication as a hallmark of a great workplace. What this means is that leaders give straight answers when asked questions, and employees believe they are approachable. You might think of accessible communication as the ways in which employees can shape and clarify the messages of the leader. Together, these communication pieces make up two-way communication, but they are worth looking at one at a time.

Informative Communication

Employees in great places to work receive informative communication through many different vehicles. On the part of top leaders, we see all-hands meetings that are well attended, we see newsletter columns and blogs, and we see verbal updates such as blast voicemail messages and webcasts. We also see creative and energizing presentations of information, like in the following two examples:

- Google, the Internet search company located in Mountain View, California, is now famous for their TGIF meetings, where cofounders Larry Page and Sergey Brin provide an informal preview of the week to come, a recap of the week's events, and a forum to ask questions (which, incidentally, also increases employees' sense of accessibility on the part of these leaders). One of Larry and Sergey's founding beliefs was that employees have the right to know what's happening at the company. TGIF meetings are webcast around the globe and archived for those in different time zones.

- Each month at JM Family Enterprises, a diversified automotive company located in Deerfield Beach, Florida, individual business units conduct 20-minute meetings for associates called "Live Monthly Events." The business unit president and senior management team members host each meeting with frequent appearances by JM Family's CEO. The meetings are videotaped and occasionally tied to a monthly theme such as Cinco de Mayo. The opening consists of industry updates, followed by a brief business unit summary. Other parts of the program include upbeat news, wherein photos might be shared from a recent holiday event. Events conclude with business-related "fun facts," a chorus of Happy Birthday to that month's celebrants, a welcome to new associates, and a raffle for various prizes. The videos are posted on the company's intranet so associates can easily reference them in the future.

Sometimes, leaders feel that these types of high-level communications are time-consuming for everyone involved, and that the value of communicating so broadly to people is lost. We disagree. Senior leaders set the direction for the work being done in the organization, giving people a sense of accomplishment and meaning. However, we can also sympathize with the leader's plight. Sometimes, we recommend that leaders bring employees *in* to their conversations rather than going *out* to communicate. For example, Boston Consulting Group (BCG), a strategic and managerial consultancy, simulcasts its bi-annual partners' meetings on the Web so the entire staff can learn from the discussions directly. In these meetings, partners review the state of the firm, share breakthrough ideas with one another, and learn from outside speakers. Not only do BCG leaders save the time it would take to summarize and

report out on the partners' meetings, they increase employee perceptions that all the information needed is available and unedited.

While BCG's example is a technological way of letting everyone in
to high-level conversations, the same principle is at work when a small
group of employees is invited to senior leadership meetings, with the
understanding that this group of employees will communicate back to
the rest of the organization—both formally and informally—about what
they've learned. While it is not a substitute for direct communication,
we recommend this technique as one of many leaders may use when
working on informative communication. It is a means to streamline
time expenditure, and it fortifies employees' perceptions that they
receive the information required to do their job.

In building a great workplace, communication is not just a job for
senior management teams. In the best organizations, employees receive
informative communications from *both* senior leaders and workgroup
managers. The communication of workgroup managers may be more
tactical in nature, providing a sense of direction for the day, or week, or
month, depending upon how often a manager might hold meetings.
In some organizations, workgroup communications are an expectation
made of all managers. In other organizations, managers are given additional tools and support for their efforts to communicate directly with
employees. In either scenario, the communications of workgroup managers should build upon the informative communication of senior leaders.

- At Atlanta-based law firm Alston & Bird, every administrative
  department and practice group joins in a daily ten-minute dialog
  called "TE Time," where TE is short for "Top Echelon." TE Time
  helps team members set a common game plan and goal for the
  day. Each day's TE Time also focuses on a different Standard of
  Service Excellence message to be incorporated into daily work habits firm-wide.

- Wegmans uses a "Meeting In a Box" to equip managers to communicate directly with their teams about issues that affect the entire organization. Meeting boxes include talking points, videos, FAQs, and tools for gathering feedback from employees. Topics often covered in these meetings are messages from the Wegman family and senior leaders about the core business or other important topics like benefits or the state of the company.
- As a part of Microsoft's focus on manager support, the Manager Portal was launched. This intranet site is designed to assist managers with employee communications, providing them with comprehensive information on critical topics, so that they are able to address any employee questions and concerns.

The biggest mistake we see leaders make when addressing the area of informative communication is to simply communicate *more often*, without considering either the best vehicles or the type of information being communicated. For instance, in retail outlets and hospitals, where there is not time to sit down and read, employees may benefit from quick and streamlined communications. Stand-up meetings and huddles are common at the best companies in such industries. Sending a memo to employees in these work environments or scheduling a lengthy meeting may be a useless effort at best, and frustrating at worst. At the best workplaces, leaders take into account their audience when choosing methods to communicate. At Microsoft, in addition to regular face-to-face and town hall style meetings, one leader communicates to the company's sales force—distributed across more than 90 countries—via a series of quarterly videos delivered digitally, leveraging technology to stay in touch with employees in his group across several time zones.

Moreover, employees are looking for information that matters to them, and often the translation of communications to their own function in the organization isn't intuitively obvious. We recommend that managers translate company results into the work unit of each department. Sales, an often easily tracked indicator of performance, might translate to the number of orders taken for a customer service department, the number of pallets loaded in the warehouse, and the number of transactions posted in accounts receivable. Managers are often in the best position to make information relevant to their employees.

Leaders at all levels should attend to the meaningfulness of their communications, their quantity, and their format. Of course, the most efficient and most powerful ways to communicate also incorporate the second aspect of communication at great workplaces—accessibility.

Accessible Communication

When you are a truly accessible leader, a couple things happen in the experience of employees. It may be helpful to ask yourself two questions.

First, do employees feel comfortable around you? Employees gain a sense of comfort in communicating with you when they feel as though you will respond to questions they ask, and that you are truly listening. Your non-verbals go a long way here. When employees approach you, do you smile? Turn your body toward them? Respond in full sentences?

We were working with a manager once who was very proud to show us how she had rearranged her office. She had moved her computer to the corner of her desk, so she could see people as they approached her when her office door was open. She could also keep an eye on what was happening on e-mail while talking with people. "So, what happens when an e-mail comes in and someone is in your office?" we asked. She proudly reported that she could keep an eye on things and communicate directly with employees at the same time. While she had the right intention—to be more available to people—splitting her attention this way did not make employees comfortable approaching her.

We discussed with the manager how employees pay attention to how available you are to them, not only physically, but emotionally and cognitively too. We also talked over ways in which she could help employees feel at ease by visiting them at their workstations rather than inviting them to come to her office, a location replete with distractions like e-mail messages and phone calls. As you consider how you will make yourself more accessible, consider making changes for the purpose of increasing employees' comfort in approaching you.

While paying attention to non-verbals can be a challenging way to answer the "comfort" question in the affirmative, another way is to simply have fun with employees. For example, the CEO of Quicken Loans uses the PA system to keep team members informed of breaking news. But the CEO most frequently uses the PA in order to give away tickets to concerts and sporting events. During "Ticket Window Thursday," the CEO uses the PA system to invite employees to call his extension to win tickets to concerts and sporting events. Similar to a radio contest, caller number "x" wins and then is interviewed over the PA system by the CEO. Hearing their leaders in such candid and frequent interactions with employees creates the sense of approachability.

Now for the second question. Do employees feel as though you are honest and—here's the daunting part—appropriately vulnerable? If you share only facts, employees may not find you as accessible as they could. Sharing opinions, emotions, and your hopes for the future indirectly invites employees to do the same. It also increases the degree of accessibility embedded in the communication.

Consider the following fact: "Profits hold steady this quarter." Now consider how a leader might communicate about that to increase his accessibility. "Profits hold steady this quarter. While I'd have loved to see us achieve some of the growth we planned for this year, I am comfortable with our numbers. Our industry has been hit hard, and I see you doing all you can to overcome some of the challenges in the marketplace.

Our goals for the year are unchanged, and I'm cautiously optimistic that we'll be able to achieve them with our new production process. It will take your hard work, and mine." Though the leader in this example has engaged in purely one-way communication at this point, he sets the stage for an honest conversation with people by sharing his reactions to the news and his hopes for the future.

Many leaders host breakfast or lunch with employees in order to create a casual atmosphere where conversations can naturally unfold. But, whether over a meal or not, when leaders directly answer the toughest questions, they make themselves vulnerable and create irrefutable evidence that they are accessible. At his town hall meetings with home-office associates, and at the end of his video updates, Jim Weddle, Edward Jones' Managing Partner, goes live to answer associate questions. "Jim is on an open-mike format during his Q&As. That is as brave as any managing partner could be," says Beth Cook, a partner responsible for Associate Relations. "People have a vehicle to ask hard questions. They might not hear an answer they want to hear, but that's business. Any issue is open to discussion. It may not be open to change or abandonment or implementation—but it is open to discussion. I think that's the best you can ask for."

Informative and accessible communication is not easy, even in the most conducive environments. Leaders in organizations that are relatively small, with one location, don't have an easy road ahead of them as far as improved communication is concerned. But leaders in large, multilocation organizations have an even tougher task. Leaders who have mastered two-way communication in such large organizations use several techniques to make sure that all employees, no matter their location or function, are well informed.

One theme we see in geographically dispersed organizations is to simulcast and record information, and make it available to people as soon as possible after its initial release. A second theme is to actively push communications and meetings down to the location or department level. Consider the following examples of strong communication in multi-location companies:

- After Adobe announces quarterly financial results, senior executives meet with the financial community regarding Adobe's performance and the next quarter's outlook. This conversation is broadcast live over the Internet for all employees and other interested parties to hear. A recording of the call is made available for a limited time on Inside Adobe, Adobe's intranet, so employees can listen to it at their convenience.

- To promote stronger senior leadership accessibility, eBay, a leader in mobile commerce and the world's largest online marketplace, developed "Chats with CEO." Using a webcast on their internal intranet, the event is watched live and on-demand by thousands, both in the U.S. and worldwide. In a relaxed, talk-show format before a live studio audience, an informal conversation is held with senior leaders about their priorities for the coming year. And, in an effort to address controversial topics head on, the host shows provocative news headlines related to the business and challenges senior leaders for their candid responses. After the session completes at the one-hour mark, executives continue the conversation by having a no-holds-barred chat session with the 200-member studio audience. To reach as many people as possible, the session's location is rotated throughout eBay's global facilities.

- Each business unit of The MITRE Corporation, an IT consulting company based in McLean, Virginia, has its own unique way of communicating, depending on its needs. Employees in the Center for Connected Government (CCG), for example, are widely dispersed at customer organizations. So CCG designated Fridays as an unofficial "homeroom" day when CCG also sponsors two optional technical forums: the Program Integration Forum, which focuses on program-customer news and information, and Brown Bags lunchtime "tech talks" that focus on "state-of-technology" topics. The lab manager also frequently arranges afternoon demos by vendors in CCG's Enterprise Technology lab.

Two-way communication is arguably the most important dimension of the Great Place to Work Model. It's not all that is needed, but it is foundational to employee perceptions of credibility, respect, fairness, pride, and camaraderie. It spills over into every aspect, including our next: competence. Consider that rarely are leaders in organizations incompetent. More often, leaders believed to be incompetent have *failed to communicate well*. How can you believe your leaders are competent in the first place if you have no idea what they're up to?

COMPETENCE

Perceived competence is the employees' belief that their leaders know what they are doing. But what does it really mean to "know what you're doing"? For one, employees believe that competent leaders coordinate resources appropriately, which includes appropriate hiring practices. They believe that leaders let people do their jobs without micromanaging. And they believe that leaders set the course for the future through vision. If employees don't believe leaders know where they're going, they are unlikely to follow them, at least for very long. As a leader, you must demonstrate the competence that you bring to the table, and thereby earn the trust of your employees.

Coordination

When employees comment on their leaders' abilities to coordinate, they discuss three main topics. The first is hiring. Of course, employees care about the top leaders who are hired, as these people can have a great deal of impact on the employee experience. But employees also care that there are processes and philosophies that ensure great hiring *throughout* the organization.

At Zappos.com, an online retailer based in Nevada, leaders acknowledge that there are occasions when people slip through the hiring process who are not cultural fits. Because having the right person in all positions is important, Zappos.com will make what is called "The Offer" during the four-week Customer Loyalty Training. At the end of the second week of training, which all new hires go through, employees are given the option to resign and get a $2,000 resignation package. Zappos.com does not want people to feel they have to stay in a position due to financial reasons; they want people to work there because they love it. By offering a resignation package of $2,000 after the new employee experiences Zappos.com, leaders hope that the new hires will evaluate whether or not Zappos.com is truly right for them. Zappos.com leaders feel that "The Offer" is actually more beneficial to the employees who don't take the package, as it ensures that everyone working with them is committed enough to give up an easy $2,000 to continue working at the company.

The second signal of good coordination is when things run smoothly—when leaders have assigned and coordinated resources intelligently both from a financial and a people perspective. The best practices when it comes to coordination rely upon both heavy involvement from the people who are carrying out the work, and communication. Sometimes, the leader's responsibility is to make the decision; other times, it is to implement the suggestions of employees.

Milliken, a textile, carpet, and chemical manufacturer located in South Carolina, has a safety process that is completely "owned" by production associates—not by management. The associates performing the work on the production line plan safety meetings, perform safety audits, and make improvement recommendations to leadership. Management's only role is support of those recommendations and the removal of obstacles that prevent a safe working environment.

Whether the company is a manufacturer or a retailer, employees are the ones who feel the brunt of ineffective or inefficient processes, staffing shortages, or resource misalignment. Help employees to understand decisions with regard to resourcing, and you'll go a long way to building perceptions of competence. Better yet, as in the case of Milliken, rely upon the expertise of employees in decisions.

The third signal of a leader's coordination ability is good decision making. Employees look at the proficiency of their leaders in making decisions for the business and providing clear leadership. In large part, the companies recognized as great workplaces are financially successful, and that is for good reason. Employees in great companies often talk about the health of their company, financially and otherwise, and their leaders' role in that success as one aspect of their great workplace. To employees, business success is a measure of a leader's competence. Yet, leaders can be viewed as competent even in financial downturns. In tough times, employees believe their leaders to be competent if they are able to explain what is happening and why it is happening, and articulate a plan for moving forward.

Oversight

In the best companies, employees feel as though they are assigned meaningful work. This is partly a framing issue; leaders communicate in ways that allow employees see their work as part of something larger. But it's also a tactical issue. Once people believe their leaders are assigning them meaningful responsibilities, they need to feel a sense of autonomy in getting the important work done. As an employee from Hoar Construction put it, "I feel like the leaders within this organization give you the training you need to do your job above and beyond, and then they let you go. They let you do it. It really motivates you because you really have the ability to make the decisions within your job description. You don't have somebody constantly looking over you and micromanaging you. They trust you. You know that when they give you that type of responsibility, it makes you feel good to know that they've given you their full confidence."

In most companies, a sense of ownership is accomplished by providing clear direction, training, and support organization-wide. If any of these things is not in place, people may not feel a healthy sense of autonomy. Yet, the immediate supervisor may also be to blame when employees feel as though they are being watched rather than trusted. Micromanagement not only reduces the amount of time leaders spend on strategically focused issues, it damages the trust employees have in their direct supervisor. In the best companies, managers are educated in striking the balance between supporting employees and controlling them. Organizational values and practices reinforce this balance.

As an example, several years ago, Edward Jones scrapped the idea of management-generated job descriptions in favor of "responsibility statements" (part of a philosophy called responsibility-based management, or RBM) written by the associates themselves. What this means is that associates essentially are in control of their careers—they draft their own goal statements and build them around measurable results they define, rather than basing them on daily activities. The contents are no secret—statements are available for anyone to read. "We don't tell associates exactly what they have to do, when they have to do it, how they have to do it," Managing Partner Jim Weddle says. "Instead, we make sure there is a clear understanding of what needs to be accomplished and what the results or output of each associate's work needs to be. We believe that, given the tools, training, and a clear understanding of what needs to be accomplished, good people will achieve." He adds, "With responsibility-based management, decisions are made by the people who are the experts because they are the ones doing the work. It makes us more nimble, more able to make good decisions quickly. We take more satisfaction in our work because we've assumed responsibility for it."

Vision

The last aspect of competence, vision, deals with the leader's ability to communicate the overarching direction of the company. We are most inspired when employees speak of the values of their organization—and their leader's role in upholding them—while also speaking of the company's immediate priorities. These employees feel both grounded in the heritage of the organization's values and driven to achieve the operating goals of the present moment.

Statements of values are not uncommon in organizations. In fact, we'd venture to guess that *most* companies have something resembling values statements that help to describe their cultures and approaches. However, something different happens in the best companies: people understand what values look like in the context of their work, and they gain this understanding through stories, rewards, and role modeling on the part of their leaders. Leaders use values to explain their decision-making processes, and they reward employees for living those values.

At The J.M. Smucker Company, a U.S.-based food products company, training on values and culture is not only for new hires. A specific training program, called "Back to Basics," serves as a refresher course for employees who have been with Smucker for five years or more. A key focus of this program is reinforcing the company's culture and the shared responsibility everyone has in preserving that culture as Smucker continues to grow. As part of "Back to Basics," senior employees are encouraged to share "tribal stories" of company values and philosophies in action in order to pass along the important lessons learned. These stories keep alive those moments when a simple action by a Smucker employee turned into something exceptional and inspiring. Providing these real-life examples for newer employees helps to connect them with Smucker's culture and heritage.

Once employees have a solid understanding of their company's values and how they translate to the work of the organization, they are empowered to act in accordance with those values. At Stew Leonard's food stores, a policy of empowerment influences all leadership actions. Empowerment is a simple policy, yet it's the one that makes team members the most proud. Everyone at Stew Leonard's, from the president to the cart crew in the parking lot, is empowered to do whatever he or she deems necessary to ensure customer satisfaction. From answering customer queries, to replacing damaged goods, to rejecting a truckload of merchandise because it doesn't meet standards, each and every team member has the authority to make decisions in his or her job without approval from the management chain.

Vision means that employees are helped to understand the more tactical priorities for the organization, and their role in achieving them. Whole Foods Market holds annual regional Vision Days for a region's leadership, Team Leaders, and Team Member representatives. Team Members of the Year are invited, as well as long-term Team Members and others who are recognized during an awards segment. Participants at Vision Day review and acknowledge the past year's accomplishments, and develop and agree upon the vision and goals for the next year. Some regions alternate their Vision Day with a regional "Future Search" event in order to set longer-term goals.

Competence is fundamental to leader credibility, but it is important to remember that it is not the fact that you and your leadership team are competent. It's that you *demonstrate* competence. You assign and coordinate resources well, involving people when possible and explaining decisions thoroughly. You and your managers support people while not micromanaging. And you repeatedly return to the values and vision of the organization to help create a clear sense of direction for employees.

INTEGRITY

Integrity is just as critical to Credibility as two-way communication and competence are, but it's uniquely difficult to distill into a set of behaviors for leaders. More than most other concepts, integrity is created through the sum total of leader behavior and an intuition about the leader's intentions. An employee's sense of his or her company's integrity is apparent in his or her answer to the question "Are my leaders reliable and ethical?"

Leaders have their work cut out for them when it comes to integrity. The general sense that leaders deliver on promises and that actions match words seems simple enough. But often, promises are implicit. As a leader, you may not even realize you've made a promise until it's broken! Or consider another aspect of integrity—the employees' beliefs that leaders would lay people off only as a last resort. Layoffs have such personal and emotional consequences that it may be difficult for people to see the logical reasoning behind them, even if they were a last resort. Lastly, perceived integrity is the sense that leaders behave honestly and ethically. Again, this is largely a matter of faith, though one based upon repeated positive and trust-building experiences with a leader.

How do leaders create such perceptions? Aside from being impeccable with their word and holding themselves to a high standard of ethical behavior, there are some actions leaders can take. Great leaders create a sense of checks and balances whereby their behavior is evaluated and feedback is given. They go to great lengths to ensure that their internal messaging matches their external messaging. And they don't sugarcoat information. In our consulting engagements, we often impress upon leaders that "You cannot talk your way out of a situation you behaved your way into." Employees must observe behavior that matches words, promises, or a general ethical standard. And, often, they must observe this match repeatedly before they extend their trust.

Reliability

Leaders in great workplaces make sure that who they are in the marketplace matches who they are internally, creating a consistent experience. And they make sure that people have an outlet to ask questions or make comments when they are confused about the integrity of decisions. These leaders make sure their words are not empty, but backed with behavior and explicit decisions on the part of the company. Leaders ensure a match between who the organization is and what they do. Two great companies provide examples of how to do this well:

- eBay uses feedback as a means to build community both inside and outside the organization. A key part of any eBay transaction is the ability to provide feedback on buyers that is visible to every other member of the online community. This feedback keeps the community strong and allows it to be largely self-regulated. Not surprisingly, employees inside the organization are encouraged to keep the culture strong through open and honest feedback. Employees are guided by eBay's values and key behaviors, and each employee knows it is his or her responsibility to give and receive feedback when those values and behaviors are not being carried out. The values are printed on their badges, and employees told us they refer to them when giving feedback to others about their behavior. Though not public feedback, eBay's expected employee-to-employee feedback gains further strength and importance because it's the same process they use—and have found effective—in the marketplace.

• Starbucks leaders established a Mission Review process to actively encourage partners to voice concerns when they believe company programs, policies, or practices are inconsistent with Starbucks's Mission Statement and Guiding Principles, or if they'd like to offer suggestions on how the company can do better. Each year, leaders receive thousands of contacts from partners, and each receives a personal follow-up, either by someone knowledgeable about the issue or topic raised, or by a member of the Mission Review team.

Reliable leaders communicate honestly, even when the news is not good. They also go to great lengths to keep their people employed during challenging financial times. Layoffs are considered a last resort, and leaders work with employees to avoid them at all costs. As one manager at SC Johnson put it, "Even though my new employees have been here a year, they're not integrated into the company yet, and they keep asking me to explain the culture to them. It's a really hard thing to sit down and verbalize. The new employees all came from publicly-held companies where, with the economic downturn, they've got friends in these companies that have lost their jobs and there have been lots of cutbacks. They're shocked by the tone management is taking here, like we're all in this together, we have to work harder, all hands on deck. There haven't been any layoffs. That's what I point to and say, 'That's the culture. I can't describe it to you other than what you're seeing and what you're experiencing.' It's been pretty interesting to see this through their eyes because I've only ever worked here." With this kind of trust in their leaders' commitment to take care of employees, people feel secure and are able to turn their attention to efforts to get out of the downturn rather than worry about their job security or the extra work they'll gain when a colleague is laid off.

Honesty

Leaders in great workplaces are honest, sometimes holding themselves to a standard of honesty that makes their PR and compliance staff members shake in their boots. At the best workplaces, leaders share the whole truth, not just the portions that are technically true and not potentially harmful to the organization. Honesty is most often tested when the company is challenged. For instance, when leaders at Nike were faced with negative press coverage about sweatshops, child labor, and non-living wages in some of their contract factories, they responded by releasing public Corporate Responsibility reports that include a full list of all contract factories Nike uses. Now, Nike commits to improving factory conditions and dedicates themselves to creating a positive social and environmental impact.

Or, consider the actions of Patrick Charmel, President of Griffin Hospital, located in Danbury, Connecticut. In late 2001, Griffin Hospital became the site of the fifth inhalation anthrax death in the U.S. Charmel received a great deal of pressure from the FBI to withhold information from employees, as they were concerned that it would then go public. However, he decided to share details with the day shift employees about what had happened. "My decision," he said "to tell employees was never in doubt even though it was personally difficult because it was in conflict with high-ranking FBI officials. I could not violate or put in jeopardy the trust relationship Griffin and I have with our employees and the community." In both cases, leaders were faced with tough decisions, and the fact that they made them both honestly and visibly increased their credibility with their employees. In this way, honesty and integrity are a leadership philosophy, and observable behavior stems from your commitment to act with honesty.

LEADER IMPERATIVES

Just because it makes good sense to focus on Credibility doesn't mean it's easy. Before we leave the conversation about Credibility, we offer a reminder of your imperatives as a leader and a behavioral checklist for managers at all levels. When working with Credibility, remember:

Function Before Form

We recommend that senior leadership teams engage in self-examination before attempting to better the relationships in their organization. You and your team need to be able to articulate where the company is going and how to get there. You need to be sure resources are deployed appropriately. You need to investigate the implicit and explicit promises being made to employees, and ensure that they are being delivered upon. Once you have verified these basics, then you may begin communicating openly with employees, and ensuring you are *demonstrating* the competence and integrity you have. Until you do so, any work on the relationships between leaders and employees is nothing more than "spin." Legitimate strategic direction, expertise, and integrity are prerequisites for building leader credibility in your organization.

Prepare for Persistence

There will be a time delay between your demonstration of credible behaviors and the benefits from doing so. Prepare yourself for it. In most organizations, short-term results are needed to justify the resources you're expending, but Credibility is an investment with a long-term payoff. The more leaders become visible, deliver on promises made in communications, and show their competence, the more people will respond. But it doesn't happen overnight. Building credibility takes commitment and persistence.

Take It from the Top

Before you begin to build credibility with the entire organization, consider the team leading it. We ask questions of top leadership teams like, "Do you trust one another?" That is, do you believe the other members of your leadership team to be credible, respectful, and fair? While questions about your senior leadership team dynamic may seem off the radar screen for the average employee, you'd be surprised at how clued in the average employee is to the team at the top. Values-based or strategic misalignments between top leaders send confusing and unreliable messages to employees. We recommend spending time determining where your team experience is positive and negative, and taking collective steps to create a great work team environment that you can both learn from and model to others. When your work team experience and efforts align with the actions you are taking at the organization level, you improve perceptions of your credibility.

The Buck Stops Here

In most leadership teams, there is one person with whom the proverbial buck stops. If there is a decision about finances on the table, though everyone may provide input, the CFO is ultimately responsible. If a new advertising campaign is being launched, the Director of Marketing holds the cards. But building credibility is everyone's responsibility. Because of the unique decision-making structure in senior teams, we often see one of two things happen. The first thing is that the credibility buck stops with HR. As we've pointed out, trust-building cannot be achieved through a people policy or program alone. While programs may be launched to create a better workplace, they only succeed if *everyone* participates and engages. The second thing we see is that no one takes responsibility. Since credibility doesn't fit neatly into any one person's role, no one champions it in meetings, and a culture of credibility evolves separately from matters of strategic importance, if at all. In both cases, any efforts to build a great workplace will fall flat. Before engaging in credibility-building, assess the dynamic of your leadership team, and come to an understanding about the means by which you will ensure that the "how" builds trust no matter "what" you are deciding upon.

Walk the Talk

Managers whose leaders engage in two-way communication are more likely to communicate with their own people. Managers see the benefit of doing so firsthand, and they have an understanding of how two-way communication is best carried out in the organization. Likewise, when managers feel fully utilized, they are more likely to aim for the full utilization of their people. And the list goes on. Leaders in the best companies don't ask people to do anything they wouldn't do themselves, and sometimes they take their actions to an extreme to signal how important it is to the company. Ray Davis, Umpqua Bank's CEO, considers his job to be that of accessibility to his people. He promises associates a response to e-mails the same day they are sent, and he holds important external meetings with the door open, pausing the meeting if he sees an associate walk by looking for him. Davis is also available by way of a silver phone—located in each store's lobby—with a direct connection to his line. Any question, from a customer or associate, is acceptable and encouraged. As a manager at Umpqua, it is much harder to skirt your associates' questions when the CEO is responding to them by day's end.

Be Predictable

When employees know where you are coming from, and they under-stand how your perspective leads to business success, it can improve the individual employee's productivity. The more predictable you are, the less time employees spend anticipating your moves or reactions to their moves, and the more work they get accomplished. Consider a group of directors we met with before working with their bosses—the senior leadership team. The directors gave us example after example of how difficult it was to work with the senior group, both because the senior group needed to approve virtually everything that the directors did, and because their opinions on things were so wildly unpredictable. Something that was a good idea yesterday may not be today. The senior group's opinions on what would make the company successful seemed to be reactions to the previous day's numbers rather than a clear direction and a solid set of values. Not only were the senior leaders damaging perceptions of their own credibility, they were also negatively affecting the productivity of their directors. While predictability may sound boring, it actually allows your employees to do the good work that will make your company successful. Individual productivity improves when leaders show themselves to be credible.

CREDIBILITY BEHAVIORAL CHECKLIST

As we've emphasized, trust in general, and credibility in particular, take time to build. Communicating regularly, demonstrating competence, and acting with reliability and integrity are key. So are the behaviors on the checklist that follows:

Two-Way Communication
- I actively welcome and respond to questions.
- I freely share information with people to help them do their work.

- I give people a clear idea of what is expected of them.
- I make an effort to talk informally with people every day.
- I regularly share information with people about our industry, operations, and financials.
- When I communicate general information about the industry or our company to people, I also illustrate what it means to them.

Competence

- I am aware of the abilities and capacity of people who work in my department and workgroup and ensure that they have challenging assignments and a manageable workload.
- I hold people accountable for the quality of their work.
- I let people in my department do their jobs without micromanaging.
- I make decisions in a timely way.
- I openly share my vision of the future with people, and suggest ways that we may reach our goals together.
- I try to give people responsibilities that are meaningful rather than menial.
- I understand the mission, vision, and values of our organization and use this information to make and communicate my decisions.
- I take care to hire people who are both qualified and good fits with our organizational culture.

Integrity

- I follow through on my promises, large and small.
- I give people updates as to the progress of decisions and action plans.
- I role model the behavior expected of people at our organization.
- I run our department in a just and fair way, and I try to mitigate any negative consequences of decisions I must make.
- I work hard to ensure that what I do aligns with what I say.
- My actions are consistent with the values of the organization and my own public statements.

PRICEWATERHOUSECOOPERS LLP: INSPIRING EXCELLENCE

Fast Facts:

- Professional Services
- Based in New York City, NY
- Founded in 1865
- Privately held by 2,200 partners
- 29,000 employees in the United States; 160,000 in offices around the world
- List-maker since 2005; recognized internationally twenty times

PricewaterhouseCoopers (PwC) is a firm of achievers. They hire the best and the brightest, and their Chairman and Senior Partner, Bob Moritz, readily admits that he wants part of his legacy to be "a firm that our clients seek on a regular basis, far outpacing the way they seek out the competition." Many of the employees we interviewed also took pride in PwC's position in the marketplace. One told us, "When I tell people I work here, they recognize PwC immediately, and I see the positive reaction on their face. It's a reflection of the high regard of the brand. It certainly makes me proud to be associated with it." In such a results-oriented culture, one might expect to find a great deal of internal competition and a narrow focus on profit. Not so at PwC.

Behind the drive for results, the culture at PwC is values and behavior based. Strong values and consistently lived core behaviors are how employees know where their company is going, and how they will get there. PwC is a culture of teamwork and collaboration, ownership and accountability, and relationships. Yes, they are competitive, but how they compete is just as important to PwC leaders. People care about each other, about their clients, and about the community. Leaders funnel consistent messages to their employees. Staff members cooperate with one another, and they create strong bonds even though the teams they work with change often. Even Moritz, when talking about his legacy, positioned it as an effort of the entire PwC team. He made a point to say, "This is not about me. This is about the leadership team, or the partners. I am just a part of it." He went on to share that "We have our partners really engaged in this. Culture and people are everyone's responsibility. It can't be just the partners. If you look at our business model, the most interaction employees have the first couple years is not necessarily with that partner, but with the immediate supervisor. So if the partner is doing all the right things, but that supervisor is not engaged, that person is walking out the door."

The values and core behaviors also shine through the employee experience, as they talk of excellence and hard work in the same breath as teamwork and trust. "We have a culture that is very team focused," one said. "When you share a common goal of achieving something as a team, you build a bond. The people who are unsuccessful here are those that are 'all work,' and that's it. But, when people connect as individuals, care for each other, and are part of the team, when they not only strive toward a deadline, but strive toward getting to know people, and picking people up when they are down, those are the people who are successful here. How do I describe the relationship with my colleagues? They are my friends."

Looking at PwC's accomplishments, you can see each of their behaviors—investing in relationships, sharing and collaborating, putting oneself in others' shoes, and enhancing value—and the reasons why PwC employees are proud of both their standing in the marketplace and the culture their leaders have helped to create:

- Partner Connectivity calls for every partner at PwC, including senior partners, to take up to 15 staff under his or her wing and get to know them personally as well as professionally—becoming acquainted with their families, personal goals, hobbies, and interests. This is not just about coaching, but rather about building relationships and connecting to each other.

- The PwC behaviors are integrated into performance coaching and development. For example, all employees receive verbal and written feedback throughout the year based on their performance in client service teams. The feedback is structured to include specific observations about the PwC behaviors, including strengths and areas for improvement. Employees then meet with their coach on a quarterly basis to review this feedback, and identify how to build on their strengths and develop as professionals.
- Firm communications, from Bob Moritz's firm-wide messages to local market and team communications, emphasize the PwC behaviors and strive to bring them alive with inspiring examples. Town hall and team meetings include panels and emphasize storytelling and two-way dialogue on the PwC behaviors.
- Employee recognition is aligned with the behaviors—ranging from spot bonuses to the national Chairman's Award program, which spotlights outstanding examples of individuals and teams that have provided exceptional service to their clients while living the PwC behaviors. These winners are recognized nationally and in their local markets as role models and sources of inspiration.
- Even "small things" are done to reinforce the behaviors. E-mail "letterhead" for PwC includes icons that reflect PwC's values and behaviors. All partners and staff choose from several new letterhead and signature options, including an "Inspire" letterhead and several environmentally friendly "green" signature messages. This is one small, but powerful way they continually remind themselves and everyone with whom they communicate, both inside and outside the firm, of what they stand for and how they inspire each other.
- Inspired by Dr. Martin Luther King's words, PwC believes that the efforts around basic human rights can never take a holiday. As a result, they consider Dr. King's birthday as a "day on": a day to take action and to recognize that progress is their responsibility. As one example, throughout many of their offices on the holiday,

PwC hosts talented high school students from local markets and introduces them to the vast array of career opportunities that are available, not just in professional services, but in the business world in general.

PwC is a winning culture, but they care about how they win. They do so through connecting with others, putting themselves in the client's shoes, and building value through teamwork. The consistency that PwC's behaviors bring to the actions of its leadership provides people with a clear sense of direction for the organization, and a great deal of trust in leadership at every level.

GOOGLE: FINDING THE GOOGLERS IN A VERY LARGE HAYSTACK

Fast Facts:

- Information Technology—Web Search
- Based in Mountain View, CA
- Incorporated in 1998 by Larry Page and Sergey Brin
- Publically traded under the symbol GOOG
- 20,000 employees in 60 offices in 20 countries
- List-maker since 2007; recognized internationally thirty-five times

When most people think of Google's workplace, they think of stories about the Googleplex and the benefits employees receive. While Googlers (employees at Google) don't discount the importance of the perks, they are quick to tell you that Google's culture and its success are not about those things at all. Claire Johnson, VP of Global Online sales, says, "My favorite part of working at Google is being able to know and connect with talented teams around the world. Whether in Mountain View or Dublin or Sao Paulo, it's obvious that having great people with a common mission is the key to attracting other motivated, talented people and to success in our mission."

When a company is growing like Google (in 2008 they reported a 31 percent year-over-year revenue growth rate), hiring and training people becomes critical to maintaining its culture and its designation as an attractive employer. Indeed, while the unique office environment is a draw for prospective employees, the ability to work alongside smart, accomplished, and interesting people is one of the biggest attractions of all. One employee says, "This is the smartest group of people that I have hung out with since my days as a graduate student in the Stanford Math department. Here, people have a very broad intelligence. They know lots and lots of different things. They're not just great engineers. Some of them are into yoga, some of them are into this, and some of them are into that. If I put up a question on Google Miscellaneous on any subject whatsoever, I get three answers by the end of the day. There's an enormous amount of intelligence concentrated in this company, which is fun."

It's fun, but it's also business. Google's entrepreneurial culture works because they hire the best, and then empower them. "You have an equal seat at the table, and it's based on the power of your idea, not how long you've been here, tenure or title or anything," says a tenured employee. "In my first week here, I was shocked that for the product I was working on, the product manager was straight out of college. She was making decisions about delaying the product. In every other company I have worked in, it had to go up to three levels of VPs before you could say that you were pushing out the schedule. That empowerment is tremendous."

Google's hiring process finds people who are not only brilliant, but also equipped to work within its unorthodox culture. Some of the key aspects of Google's hiring process include the following:

- An online application system sifts through the millions of applications received in order to identify those with potential. Google's scientific and data-driven approach to screening helps them both to identify the candidates most likely to perform well and to channel applicants into the functional areas that are right for them.
- While ability and appropriateness to the role are evaluated, so is the candidate's ability to work within Google's culture. Candidates are assessed on their ability to work in a flat organization and on small teams, and the ability to respond to a fast-paced, rapidly changing environment. Successful candidates are passionate, they are willing to attack problems with flair and creativity, and they have enthusiasm for the challenge of making the world a better place instead of doing evil. A Googley person is ethical and communicates openly, and can be serious without a suit.

- Ever data-driven, Google seeks to make the application experience a good one for candidates through a survey called VoxPop—an abbreviation of *vox populi*, Latin for "voice of the people." The recruiting organization then uses the feedback from this survey to improve the candidate experience and to provide further training for both recruiters and interviewers.
- It wouldn't be Google if hiring weren't also fun. Google reaches out to college students through a contest called Google Code Jam, where global programmers compete to solve complex coding challenges in a limited amount of time. While not all participants are job seekers, several are, and the top 25 finishers visit Google in Mountain View for the final round of competition. So not only does Google remain current on the creations of the most talented programmers in the world, they also have a ready-made applicant pool through this unique program.

Google's leaders know that investing time and effort into hiring the right people pays off in multiple ways. Of course, good hiring anywhere results in getting people on board who can contribute to the continued success of the company. But Google also knows that hiring the right people with broad skill sets is what maintains success in the ever-changing world of technology. One employee nicely summed up the Google philosophy of hiring: "We always look less for experience because we never look for a round peg to put into a round hole. We're not looking for a shortstop on the baseball team. We're looking for people with athletic ability, lung power, and hand-eye coordination because in most cases we are going to ask them to play a sport that hasn't been invented yet. I've seen people being hired to work on ads, and all of a sudden, who knew that we'd be in another business? You have to be very versatile. You can only hire broad generalists with certain skills or attributes. The kind of things we look for are how smart and intelligent they are in a broad sense, the curiosity thing, and if they have a diverse set of interests.

Case Study

Case Study

If you come in and say that you are the origami world champion or the aerobics world champion, that's a big deal because it shows you excelled in something and you have a passion and intensity."

Not everyone can work for Google, but lots of people want to. Google's leaders know that paying attention to hiring helps them succeed, and helps them maintain their designation as a great place to work.

CHAPTER THREE

RESPECT

"I am a valued member of this organization."

Not every suggestion I've made over the years has been implemented—but I've always felt like I was heard and I've always felt like I was empowered to share the feedback. Heck, my current position and the one before that are jobs that I basically created because I saw an essential issue that needed to be addressed. Both times, a department has grown up out of it and is still in operation.

—EMPLOYEE AT SAS

G o to any company's website, and search for their "core values." You will likely see "respect" listed as one of them. And yet if you take a moment more and read through what a handful actually write about respect, you will quickly find a lot of variation in how management teams define it. For example, one company defines the value as "we communicate to one another with mutual respect, and acknowledge each other as important players on the team, irrespective of profession or position," and another offers that "every associate deserves to be treated with respect, and to treat others in the same manner. The company is committed to creating a work environment based on mutual respect and dignity"—which really says a lot and not very much at the same time.

Most organizations understand that creating a respectful work environment and holding people to account for the maintenance of such an environment is a bottom line requirement. Organizations are able to more effectively gain employee commitment for a task or team-work on a project when there is an environment of respect. Little wonder, then, that organizations talk about and aspire to having respectful workplaces.

In great workplaces, though, respect is more than a requirement. If you want to know what areas of an organization *really* signal respect, the quote at the top of the chapter from the SAS employee is a good place to look. This employee's comment offers us several markers of how respect manifests itself in the best workplaces. First, respect is not getting one's own way all the time, but it is always having one's ideas and needs affirmed. Even when this employee doesn't get what she wants, at least she has been heard, which fosters a spirit of cooperation and collaboration. Second, this employee is empowered to take risks, innovate, and create on behalf of the business. She has the ability to make choices and be involved with meaningful work. As a result, she has been able to stretch herself, grow and develop in her career, and provide substantive value back to the organization.

True respect of the sort this SAS employee tells of is critical, and is the second of the three building blocks of trust we wrote about in Chapter 1. Without respect, you simply can't have trust, and without trust, you can't have a great workplace. Leaders set the tone for how employees and their contributions are viewed, which is the essence of Respect. Great workplaces see and value the needs that employees have beyond their specific job and work to address the "whole person." A respectful workplace requires leaders to demonstrate a sincere interest in workers as people, not just as employees. For example, it might be thanking an employee for a job well done—in the way in which *they* most value being appreciated.

The challenge for you as a leader is to get practical about what respect is and is not in the workplace, and then go about the business of breaking down obstacles and leveraging existing opportunities for building a respectful workplace. This chapter aims to take you from the general idea of "respect" to how it operates in some very specific ways in best companies, and to show how you can influence the development of respect in your organization. Respect is not a "nice to have"; it is a business imperative in today's environment.

We all can think of a manager who had great business skills but lacked any empathy or ability to work with people. And we can probably also think of a manager who was a great "people person" but just wasn't adept at managing the business. Managerial success requires both. An employee at one of our clients recounts how, at a former employer, she dreaded getting out of bed in the morning and usually had a pounding headache by the time she reached the company's parking lot. She felt like she was always set up to fail by her company, and that her manager really didn't care about her success. Getting her manager to authorize the training necessary to do her job was a hurdle; he would shift her responsibilities without warning or her input, and he never even said "hello" to her, let alone asked how she was. And she was in customer service. She was miserable. How do you think her customers felt?

On the other hand, ensuring that employees are given the training they need and involving them in decisions that impact their work creates both competence and commitment. As customers or clients, we tend to appreciate it when the person we are interacting with seems competent in assisting us and eager to do so. Companies such as Nordstrom and Four Seasons are known for their exemplary customer service. They are also great workplaces. This is not a coincidence; instead, managers in these organizations work to demonstrate a high level of respect for their people, and their people in turn understand what it means to demonstrate respect to their customers. FedEx sums this up nicely with their "PSP," or "people, service, profit" philosophy. Take care of your people, and they will deliver great service to customers, which will result in a healthy profit. It can be a virtuous cycle, but it does require managers to show genuine respect for their people.

Respect impacts more than customer satisfaction, however. Creativity and innovation flourish when people are actively involved in brainstorming, thinking together, and making decisions, and when they are accountable for following through. When people know that they can take a calculated risk on behalf of the business, and their manager will support them even when an honest mistake is made, innovation increases even more. And the benefits of respect don't stop there. Employee involvement in the decision-making process increases employees' understanding of why decisions are made and helps people to appreciate management's decision-making responsibilities. Employees develop a deeper sense of ownership in their work and responsibility for successful implementation of changes because they share in the decisions about how their work gets done.

All of these are important benefits. As a leader, demonstrating respect to employees yields significant dividends back to you as you benefit from a more aligned, connected, engaged, and committed workforce.

There are three main areas that affect an employee's perception of respect at his or her organization. The first is support. Support is manifested in the way managers support individuals' professional worth, through offering training and professional development, and through ensuring that people have the resources they need to do their job. Support also takes the form of appreciating an employee's extra effort and recognizing his or her accomplishments. The second area employees look to is a sense of collaboration or involvement in decisions that impact their work. And the third area employees note in a respectful relationship is a genuine sense of caring. Let's explore these ideas of support, collaboration, and caring a little deeper.

SUPPORT

Support in the best companies typically focuses on ensuring that employees have opportunities to grow and develop, that they have the necessary resources to conduct their work, that their contributions are recognized and appreciated, and that honest mistakes are not held against them. When we talk with employees in great workplaces, they say things like:

- The owners are very involved—more so than at any other company I have worked for. They work very hard to show appreciation to the employees and give back to the employees and the community.
- I feel that the company truly cares about their employees and recognizes their efforts.
- I'm given resources even before I know I need them. They set us up to be successful.

Supporting Professional Worth

We talk a lot with our consulting clients about "setting people up for success." Two fundamental ways a manager can really set a person up for success are by 1) thinking comprehensively about the type of development this person requires, and 2) getting him or her the right tools, equipment, and other materials needed to complete his or her assigned work or accomplish agreed-upon goals. When managers work in this manner, employees are more likely to have a sense of meaningful work and professional worth.

Managers at all levels understand the value of training and developing their people. In most organizations we work with, we see a focus on job skills training—training to "skill up" employees to do a specific job, task, or project requirement. In very good workplaces, these basics are covered, but managers also support the overall career development of their people. They understand that as the business continues to grow, they will need employees who can readily step into tomorrow's job rather than having them develop necessary skills on the fly, hiring from outside, or simply losing the market opportunity. The better course is to understand the hopes, talents, and aspirations of one's employees, and actively work toward aligning those interests with future business needs. Managers can use a broad range of activities to support this type of development, including external classes and degree programs, professional conferences, online programs, coaching and mentoring, certifications, and internships or externships.

Here are some examples of these programs in practice:

- During their second month at Microsoft, employees attend a second orientation course to spend time discussing their experience to date, a financial overview, and talent management. The course, along with a question-and-answer period, is intended to help newer employees understand their learning curve, the structure of the business, performance review processes, and career development opportunities. The course helps them put into context any emotional ups and downs they may experience.
- The LVN to RN program was first created and implemented at Scripps Memorial Hospital in Encinitas, allowing employees to complete self-study modules to obtain their associate's degrees in nursing while working either full-time or part-time. Today that program has evolved to encompass a system-wide approach to education, and in particular clinical education, that includes tuition reimbursement programs, scholarships, partnerships with local schools, and loan programs that allow Scripps staff to move into nursing, allied professional positions, and other critical-to-fill jobs. As an example, the Scripps Clinical Education Loan Scholarship program gives employees financial assistance in return for two years of service in critical-to-fill positions. Each location's program

supports a "grow our own" philosophy of talent development, and they provide employees with educational opportunities to move into professional-level positions, which is a winning proposition for both Scripps and the employees.

These companies provide several specific ideas, but there are more. We've seen managers go beyond what is available from the company or local community by engaging in one-on-one discussions with employees about their career goals and aspirations, debriefing the learning activities they experience in training, and helping them apply their new insights into business challenges.

Managers can take an active role and seek out opportunities for employees to apply their new skills, develop their careers, and seek promotions. At W. L. Gore & Associates, part of the role of sponsors (they don't have bosses or managers at Gore) is to look at the internal job board for their associates and suggest new job opportunities. Managers can host "lunch and learn" programs wherein team members read a relevant article or book and discuss the implications for a project or team. But what underlies all of these creative ways to support employees' career development is that managers not only put into place supportive practices, they commit their own time and energy into making these practices successful.

An employee from Gore (we'll call him John) provides a terrific example of what can happen when managers take note of natural leadership in entry-level employees and help translate it into formal leadership roles. John is a thoughtful, humble guy, and he has become a leader and go-to person in his tenure at Gore. Over the course of his tenure, John has learned some valuable lessons about how to be a leader. He recounts an important lesson he learned in supporting others' growth:

> When I first started, I was in housekeeping. My routine was to
> clean and keep everything neat and tidy, and I worked on the

off-shift. I had a leader in the area and he would always say, "Production is where you want to be. When you have free time and you're done with your work, stop by the production floor and buddy up with somebody. See how everything works. See how the processes work." I would do that. I found a friend who was working in production. When I was done cleaning, I would go over and hang out and talk and watch them work. One day, she put me to work. She said, "If you're going to stand here and talk to me, you're going to run this piece of equipment!" This was before computers, so she made me sign the paperwork and everything. One day, they had their operations meeting, and somebody raised the question, "Who is JJ? We keep getting this paperwork with JJ on it, and we have no one in production named JJ!" After they got done, they came back and said, "Can we speak with you? We have some equipment that JJ's been running and you're the only JJ we know." I explained what had happened about them giving me the opportunity to work. It wasn't until later that some openings came up and my leader said, "You are putting in for this job, right?" We talked for a long period of time, and I finally put in for the job, and I got the job. I probably did housekeeping for about 2 years, and I've been working in production in the fabrics division for about 19 years. It's been just great to see how people look at you and see something in you and give you a chance and point you in the right direction. It's been great.

In this story, John is not a passive player. Supporting the development of employees does not mean handing over their next promotion; it is truly supporting employees in their *own* growth and development. In the example, John networked with other people and remained open to learning, adjusting, growing. However, he did have support from leadership, and they were mindful of his career trajectory as they sourced for a new position. John's story is not unique in best companies. Leaders in great workplaces anticipate opportunities for their people.

They understand that growing their people equates to growing the organization, and in today's global economy, companies that are not actively growing are actually shrinking.

Beyond formal training, an additional aspect of support is giving employees space to create and invent. Examples abound in the information technology industry:

- At Google, the 20 percent project is a unique program that encourages engineers to spend 20 percent of their time on projects outside their typical work responsibilities. This allows engineers to put energy into ideas that could potentially benefit the company. Encouraging continuous innovation enables employees to recharge their creative energies while simultaneously broadening their knowledge base.

- Creativity and innovation are a critical part of Microsoft's culture. In an effort to make sure all employees have an opportunity to explore their creative side, Microsoft started Mashup Days. Mashup Days offer every employee the opportunity to share creative ideas about products. The event consists of fun, creative brainstorming sessions, where every voice is heard, and every idea noted. In addition to generating ideas, employees at Mashup Days also seek feedback on test products.

In many of the best companies, "life development" programs are included along with traditional job or career development programs. They provide employees a chance to understand more about specific issues that impact their lives outside of work. For example:

- During Quicken Loans' 45-Day Challenge for Life Balance, team members are led through a process of self-discovery over the course of a month and a half. The program focuses on personal development, and spouses or partners are invited to participate. Through the program, daily homework exercises and weekly seminars help participants evaluate themselves on four key areas: mindset, career, relationship, and energy. Team members find the program challenging, difficult, and extremely rewarding as they grow in their careers and relationships.

• Milliken, a textile manufacturer based in Spartanburg, South Carolina, gives associates the tools they need to manage their lives as well as their jobs. A class is offered that teaches associates to maximize their monthly income and to reduce impulse spending using a three-step system. Participants also learn how to eliminate personal debt and how to strategize for a strong financial future.

The common thread through these examples is the respect these companies show to employees—respecting their talents and interests, respecting their hopes and aspirations, and respecting the whole person. Leaders in the best companies understand that developing people results in important dividends back to the company. As employees receive not only the learning and development required to successfully engage in their jobs but also opportunities to grow in their careers and learn important skills to manage their lives, their engagement, loyalty, and competence increase.

Supporting Individual Effort

Employees come to work with two basic career questions they want managers to answer. The first is "Where am I?" and the second is "Where am I going?" And in the best companies, managers answer those questions on a regular basis. Training and development of the sort covered in the previous section addresses the second question, but now let's turn to the first: "where am I?" Employees want to know how they are doing, and this requires ongoing feedback about their performance.

One way we see managers at the best companies providing ongoing feedback is by "catching an employee doing something right." What is really happening is that managers in these companies seek to create a climate of appreciation—one in which they consistently seek to recognize good work and extra effort, and in which they pay attention to the process of recognition. Sincere appreciation and recognition go a long way in demonstrating respect to employees. And when, on occasion, an employee makes an honest mistake, helping the employee learn from it rather than blaming the employee for the mistake signals a genuine sense of professional support.

Where you invest your time and attention as a leader serves as a powerful model for what employees see as important and meaningful. In our coaching of leaders, our experience has been that when a leader focuses time and attention on their people's successful performance behavior, employees respond with even greater energy and commitment. Publically recognizing success also demonstrates what successful performance looks like to other employees. In this way, committing to making recognition a daily habit benefits not just the single employee but everyone else as well. As consultants, we have observed that most leaders and most organizations do not do enough of this. Honestly, if you were to ask yourself "Am I thanked *too* much at work?" chances are you would say no. Most people aren't thanked enough for their contributions; instead, they are rarely praised at all for their good work and extra effort.

In terms of the process of recognition, we find that leaders at best companies consider *what* is being recognized (e.g., performance, service, philanthropy); *the means* by which it is recognized (e.g., formally, informally, peer programs); and the *rewards* themselves (e.g., cards, gifts, financial incentives).

Best companies recognize employees for going above and beyond, for their professional contributions or achievements, and for tenure or service anniversaries. They also tend to recognize behaviors that are aligned with the company's values. And most of the best companies offer recognition in areas such as client satisfaction, new product or service ideas, referrals of new people to the organization, and employees' volunteer efforts. CarMax's CEO Tom Folliard, for example, has a monthly recognition list called "Tom's Top Ten." Every month, he sends an e-mail to announce the top ten stores for the previous month. A store could earn the honor because of outstanding sales results or significant improvement in any area (e.g., number of appraisals, a new record of credit applications, increased customer conversion, etc.). Aside from bragging rights, winners receive a "big sandwich" party for all store associates, a special award signed by Tom, and recognition in the CarMax quarterly company newsletter, *On the Road*.

Leaders at best companies also carefully consider the means by which they recognize employees. The question they ask themselves is "what message am I trying to send here and to whom?" As a result, sometimes recognition is carried out in a formal or public way, such as an awards ceremony or team meeting. More often, leaders engage in informal or spontaneous recognition. In some best companies, it is not uncommon to get a thank you note or card from one's manager or a voicemail from the CEO at unexpected times. Leaders can also encourage peers to recognize one another, and in fact peer recognition programs are common in best companies. At IKEA, a home furnishings retailer, some locations offer opportunities for coworkers to say "thank you" or "job well done" to one another. "Tack" boards are posted in the hall ("Tack" is the Swedish word for "thanks") where coworkers can write messages to one another to say "thanks" or "I think you did a good job."

When placed in the hands of managers, recognition programs allow people to be recognized on the spot for good work rather than awaiting the formal appraisal and bonus process. To make the recognition and reward even more meaningful, many companies encourage managers to make the reward personal to the employee. These personalized and on-the-spot awards are often quick-wins in building trust with employees. As an example, the VP Award at Genzyme, a biotechnology company headquartered in Cambridge, Massachusetts, is an on-the-spot cash bonus program that managers can use at their discretion at any time during the year. The award is budgeted and expensed directly through the manager's operating funds. The VP award can be a small token "thank you" style award or a more meaningful award for a special project or accomplishment by a team or an individual.

Finally, leaders at best companies consider the reward itself. At some best companies, rewards can be very generous and novel; however, they need not be. As consultant Cindy Ventrice notes in her book, *Make Their Day! Employee Recognition That Works* (2009), "In an international survey in 2007, I found that 57 percent of the most meaningful recognition doesn't even cost a dollar . . . employees are looking for meaning, not things." (pg. 12) A genuine, verbal thank you can go a long way. Other programs such as time off, celebrations, and benefiting from the company's performance through programs like profit-sharing can round out the types of recognition you offer your people.

COLLABORATING WITH EMPLOYEES

Just as supporting employees is a critical step toward building Respect, so, too, is collaborating. Amy Lyman, the Great Place to Work Institute's cofounder, has observed, "Ideas are everywhere—individual ideas, group ideas, ideas that have been thought of, considered, argued over, discarded or never fully considered. There's no shortage of ideas. Gaining access to ideas, developing and selecting them, and putting the best ones into action—making decisions, choosing among alternatives—those are the real challenges." In best companies, leaders demonstrate respect by gaining access to employees' ideas, developing them, and ensuring that employees know how their input was used.

Ideas are indeed everywhere, and managers at best companies continually seek out suggestions for business problems. They seek to understand the likely impact of business decisions on the employee experience. They employ two basic but important skills: they ask questions, and they listen. Significantly, they invest time and energy into ensuring that their questions are the right ones; the quality of the answers depends on that. Rather than asking a casual, unformulated question, these managers carefully consider what needs finding out. In fact, in many best companies, "useful questions" are provided to managers for use in employee meetings, or managers will come together and discuss what those questions are. For example, Baptist Health Care performs "rounding," where managers walk the floors with the intent of finding out answers to several key questions, and then the managers come together to review what was discovered.

Another example of a collaborative idea exchange comes from the retailer Eileen Fisher (EF). They formed a leadership system called the Leadership Forum, consisting of 21 key leaders across the company who meet every three weeks for most of a day to share information, discuss key issues, and make decisions or recommendations. In 2007, the Leadership Forum designed new ways to ask questions of their Eileen Fisher community. One of these ways was by inviting "guests" to join Leadership Forum meetings. These guests (four to five people) from various EF teams are included as full members of the forum on a meeting day—they participate in the check-in process and provide comments and feedback throughout the day's conversations. Not only do the guests gain greater insight to the company but also the meetings help to build strong relationships between leaders and people in the company. Note how similar this practice is to that of BCG in the previous chapter. Both companies invite employees into the meetings of top-level leaders in the organizations. Seeking ideas also helps to create a perception of credibility through two-way communication.

Our experience with clients tells us that often managers shy away from seeking input or opinions because they are uncertain about what to do with the data they receive. How does one process all of this information and make sense of it? One of the first steps is to provide managers and employees with the right skills, structure, and opportunity to engage in collaborative decision making. Amy Lyman suggests that "Two specific skills that, when practiced well, can greatly enhance people's ability to work well together are those of practicing positive dissent and providing constructive criticism." Encouraging positive dissent means making a fundamental challenge to the idea being put forward, usually based on overarching values or goals. On the other hand, the goal of constructive criticism is to provide the decision maker (be it a leader or a team member) with helpful critiques along the way. When leaders have these skills, they are better able to hear ideas, because they know they can positively dissent when employees provide input, and constructively criticize ideas when they are not in the decision-making seat.

Many best companies offer specific training on how to provide feedback and engage in such constructive criticism, which in turn enables their leaders to be better collaborators. Robert W. Baird provides training on "crucial conversations," while Boston Consulting Group provides managers with extensive training on giving feedback. All associates at W. L. Gore & Associates take a core communications program that highlights the use of "I messages" in giving feedback. In all of these ways, best companies equip employees with the tools and knowledge to be involved. And employees, in return, feel respected for their knowledge and contribution.

Many best companies have structures in place that encourage collaboration. Several examples follow:

- W. L. Gore & Associates has a set of guiding principles they refer to as a means of reinforcing their decision-making process. For every decision that needs to be made, associates look to their principles (commitment, freedom, fairness, and waterline). When new patent concepts are proposed, they are reviewed with questions like: Who will be driving it? Do the appropriate associates have the freedom to participate? Is the decision fair to the team affected and the business? Will it affect any trade secrets? In this manner, they use their principles to provide the necessary structure for collaboration and effective decision making.

- QUALCOMM is a communications technology firm located in San Diego, California, and innovation is a critical piece of their culture. They created the QUALCOMM Innovation Network program, a Web-based "idea management system" aimed at triggering internal entrepreneurship and transforming the creative thinking of employees into valuable product ideas. This worldwide initiative includes collaboration tools (such as forums to gather feedback on ideas), lectures, resources (white papers, people, research mechanisms, and more), professional networking, and most recently, a friendly competition that invites all employees to submit business plans for evaluation by a team of executives. By creating a worldwide initiative, QUALCOMM sends a strong message to employees that they have innovative ideas the organization is interested in hearing.

- Google also provides a set of tools for managers and employees to encourage collaboration and innovation. On the "Google Ideas" website, Googlers regularly submit their thoughts on product improvements or suggestions about how to make things better around Google. Their colleagues can then weigh in by providing their feedback through comments and ratings, which range from 0 (Dangerous or harmful if implemented) to 5 (Great idea! Make it so). The management team pays very close attention and is responsive to issues that Googlers find important enough to discuss on one of their internal e-mail lists. Sometimes, the conversations started on one of these e-mail threads have become the topic of a larger discussion at a TGIF, Google's weekly company-wide get-together.

Best companies ask employees questions. They incorporate employee ideas. But those two acts aren't enough when it comes to collaborating. The third thing we consistently see at best companies is managers "closing the loop" with employees. Whether employees are a party to the actual decision-making event or not, leaders in best companies encourage a process for ensuring that employees understand the decision, its rationale, and how employee input was used and considered, and enlisting employee support for the decision. As President of Developed Markets Patrick O'Brien of SC Johnson observes, "[Locking] into core philosophies will allow the flexibility for programs to move or new products to move or business decisions to be made. I think it's really important in my role to make sure that people understand the values and the philosophies when they are presenting ideas, such as what we're going to invest in these businesses for the long-term. We've just done a ton of new products this year in one of the worst recessions ever, but those were not investments for today. They're investments so that we can be stronger over the next five to ten years. And that is a philosophy I work to make sure is understood."

CARING FOR EMPLOYEES

The third and final piece of Respect is caring for your employees. When we interview employees and ask them to identify ways in which managers demonstrate respect, more often than not they speak of the ways in which they feel cared about in the organization. Caring may seem beyond behavioral definition, but we've found it actually isn't. We look for the extent to which managers show an interest in people's well-being—by providing a safe and healthy working environment, and by providing benefits that support people's lives outside of the workplace. Caring managers are aware of the impact that work has on employees' personal lives. Says one employee at Wegmans, "When I think about leaders in the company and the managers I work with, I think of words like *care, genuineness,* and *trust*. Those are the foundation that we build our relationships on."

Work Environment

Facilities that are safe and contribute to a good working environment are an important demonstration of respect. Beyond that, however, leaders at best companies understand a very basic formula: behavior is a function of a person interacting in their environment. It follows that in order to shape performance outcomes, leaders must not only attend to the person but to the environment as well. In our visits with best companies in the U.S. and around the world, our experience has been that these companies take this maxim to a high level. At Microsoft's headquarters, the majority of the building consists of various types of meeting rooms. Some rooms resemble what you might find in your living or family room, other rooms resemble a coffee shop. There are conference rooms and classrooms, of course, but the focus there is on helping employees get together in spaces that make sense given the project or issue.

The message of respect that comes from a great physical environment is even greater when leaders involve people in the planning of their workspace. During the planning process for a new building, DreamWorks Animation conducted meetings with each department to elicit opinions on everything from workspace configurations to desk size. As a result, the design team made important modifications that would save the company money and help to create an even more aesthetically beautiful and functional environment. The opportunity to be a part of the decision-making process also gave employees a greater sense of ownership and control over their physical environment.

If you go to the SAS campus in Cary, North Carolina, or the Google campus in Mountain View, California, or the Microsoft campus in Redmond, Washington, you notice that they really do resemble a campus. They are all workplaces that engage and inspire, rather than just offer space to work. Even in bigger cities with not as much room for a sprawling park campus, best companies create physical work environments that respect the people working in those buildings. At the Genzyme Center, Genzyme's global headquarters building in Boston, the entire building was designed from the "inside out," with the comforts and effectiveness of its employees in mind. All attributes of the building—from the soaring 12-story central atrium with skylights, to the extensive indoor gardens—were designed to create the ideal workplace for their employees. The building design encourages informal meetings in the building's common spaces, garden areas, and top-floor cafeteria with its sweeping views of the Boston cityscape. Various terraces, corners, and walkways are furnished to encourage spontaneous conversations. Offices are kept small, while the amount of common space per employee is significantly greater than in a typical U.S. office building. These features help foster a higher level of interaction, collaboration, and creativity.

Another unique factor in Genzyme's environment is that the headquarters received a Platinum rating—the highest possible—from the U.S. Green Building Council, the nation's foremost authority on environmentally responsible building practices. The Genzyme Center is one of the largest corporate office buildings to earn the Platinum certification. The building uses 32 percent less water than a comparable building, and electricity costs are 38 percent less. More than 50 percent of all materials include recycled content, and more than 90 percent of all the construction waste was recycled. It is a place employees feel good about coming to work for this and other reasons. One of the important underlying aspects of all four of the companies mentioned here is the alignment of their facilities with their core values as organizations. In the case of Genzyme, innovation, transparency, collaboration, and entrepreneurial spirit are all values that can be seen represented in the physical structure of their buildings.

Work-Life Balance

As a leader, you can also demonstrate respect and caring about employees' personal lives through encouraging appropriate work-life balance and stressing the importance of taking time away when necessary. The difference between a good place to work and a great place to work is that in a good place to work, there are work-life balance practices (flex time, compressed work weeks, telecommuting, hoteling, virtual workspace, job sharing, phased retirement, and so on), but in great workplaces, you actually get to use those benefits, and are encouraged to do so! As a leader, simply having practices "on the books" does not convey a sense of respect. Encouraging employees to take time after completing a large, demanding, or intense project, or responding creatively to their at-home needs is more likely to result in a recharged and engaged employee than one who is constantly burning the candle at both ends. Some companies practice tough love when it comes to work-life balance, such as a pharmaceutical company based in Mexico City that takes a practice called "We turn off the lights" literally. In order to encourage employees to balance their personal and working lives, and also to make a better use of their personal time, all the lights of the company are turned off at 6:30 pm, except on sales closing days. There is no option for employees to turn them on again, so instead they go home or make use of the gym. But your organization need not get that prescriptive. Rather, as a leader, your attention and energy in this area is often the single biggest predictor of whether employees find balance and take care of themselves.

SAS provides a great example of fostering work-life balance. There are over 125 regular (not contracted) SAS employees whose primary function is to develop, support, and deliver ongoing programs like on-site childcare, camps, eldercare, parent education and support, financial education, a fully-equipped fitness center, on-site health care, and wellness programs. In addition, flexible work schedules and the overall work environment contribute to the satisfaction and peace of mind of SAS employees. Employees know they're working for a company that is committed to their long-term success and they, in turn, are committed to the long-term success of the company. The on-site Health Care Center has a 56-member staff, and there is no appointment cost or co-pay to employees or their covered dependents. The on-site Recreation and Fitness Center also offers complimentary access to employees, family, and domestic partners. The center offers numerous swim, aerobic, and athletic classes; arranges intramural leagues in various sports; and organizes family and individual trips and activities at SAS and in the community. For regional office employees who are too far away to take advantage of the main campus facilities, the company pays for fitness center memberships.

SAS is a large company, but even smaller best companies invest in programs and policies that encourage employee balance and wellness. Lincoln Industries is a small manufacturing company based in Lincoln, Nebraska. Simply, their respect for "the whole person" is woven into the very fabric of their company, and it manifests itself in many unique benefits for their people. The company has a Wellness Program nationally recognized by the Wellness Council of America, and when it first earned the Platinum Award in 2003, it was only one of twelve companies in the nation to do so. The program strives to make wellness fun with contests, special events, and activities that allow its people to practice healthy habits, which contribute to a healthier company. Though the program is fun in spirit, the company also takes it seriously. It mandates each person be checked quarterly for changes in weight, body fat, flexibility, and blood pressure. Personal goals are established jointly with the Wellness Manager, monitored throughout the year, and included in the job performance review process. While there is an organizational focus and staff dedicated to wellness, managers play an important role in encouraging employees to get involved and stay active. And managers themselves model the types of balance and wellness behaviors that are expected.

Sincere Interest

On our Trust Index survey, one of the statements that is most highly correlated with whether employees perceive their company as a great workplace is whether their manager takes a sincere interest in them as people. It might be helpful here to remember that the employee perspective counts. It's not simply *that* you care about employees, it's that you *show* you care about employees.

Bob, an employee at Wegmans, recalls, "I remember coming here 29 years ago. I was a cashier, and I would get my till and go to the desk to see where I was going, and it was always preceded with maybe a minute-long conversation of, 'How are you? How's school? Your schedule working out well?' I think that kind of caring starts from the top. If we get visits from our corporate leadership it always starts with those personal questions. And it ends with those personal questions. And in-between there's business. So we do those things exceptionally well at Wegmans, and it keeps it going." In best companies, managers "take the extra 60 seconds" to check in with people, get to know them, and remember specifics about their personal lives.

Years ago, at W. L. Gore & Associates, founders Bill Gore and his wife, Vieve, would visit the plants on a regular basis, and before they went, they would be provided with a book with everyone's photos and names so that they knew who they were talking to. It never ceased to impress the associates at Gore. Contrast that with the kind of stories we hear regularly, which probably sound familiar, of employees encountering leaders in the hallway and the leader not even saying "hello" or acknowledging them.

As a leader, discovering more about your people and remembering to ask about someone's son's little league game can go a long way. As a manager at SC Johnson offers, "When I moved into this new group, one of the first things I did was to schedule one-on-ones with every single person in my department. I think people really responded to that, and they thought that was refreshing. You come into the job and the first thing the manager does is just sit down with everybody and the first discussion is just to get to know people. I just want to get to know people as people. That's something that I learned from this company."

Special and Unique Benefits

While we see a lot of differences among the best companies, one of the commonalities the employees' sense is that their company is special and unique. And one of the ways employees tend to experience that sense of being special and unique is by receiving benefits that an employee might describe as "only here." A couple of examples follow:

- Green Mountain Coffee Roasters, a medium-sized company based in Waterbury, Vermont, offers employees an all-expenses-paid trip to a coffee-producing country. Twenty percent of all employees had taken this trip at the time of the company's first nomination to our list. Returning travelers share pictures, memories, and stories of their trips. The goal of these trips is to build and maintain relationships between the company and its source partners. In the words of one leader, "There is nothing like trying to pick coffee beans on steep hillsides in the rainforest to help an employee understand how much work goes into growing great coffee."
- REI offers "challenge grants" to employees. Challenge grants provide up to $300 in REI-brand gear and apparel to help employees

achieve their own outdoor recreation goals, such as competing in a triathlon or scaling a peak. This benefit is designed to encourage outdoor exploration, which is the basis of REI's retail business.

At their foundation, these programs are about *caring* for the individual and the community. They fit within the context of that company's culture, and the message to employees is that "you are a part of us," which in the end is what people want to know from you: that they matter.

LEADER IMPERATIVES

First, a story. Jack DePeters, Wegmans' Senior Vice President of Operations, recounts a story that brings together several key themes of respect. "Bob Wegman once asked our stores to slice and display deli meats in a certain way, but it wasn't being done the way he had envisioned. No matter which store, the deli people were struggling to make it happen. A part-time employee by the name of Beth came up to the store manager and said, 'I think I know what he wants; will you let me do it?' At the same time she was in a bit of financial trouble and the utility company had turned her heat off. It's cold here in Rochester. One of her coworkers happened to drive by Beth's home, saw it was dark, asked a few questions, and finally she broke down and said she couldn't afford her gas and electric bill. The store manager found out about it, wrote a check from our Spirit of Giving Fund, and paid her bill in full. When Bob Wegman came in the next time, the deli display was done just as he wanted it. He was very excited and thanked the store manager, who brought Beth out. Bob gave her one of his big hugs, and she said, 'Thank you Bob, for all you've done,' and he said, 'Beth, we're even.'"

Create a Climate of Mutual Respect

Remember the prerequisite of being genuinely caring and authentic? The manager respects his people. Beth wants to matter and make a difference at work, and her manager gives her that opportunity. There is some degree of collaboration, and ultimately he supports her in making the necessary changes to the display. Around the same time, the manager also found out about what was going on for her at home and he acted. He saw her need and addressed it. And when the owner, Bob Wegman, goes to recognize him, he stops him so that the credit is redirected to the person who really earned it. The manager showed respect for Beth, both as an employee and as a person, and in return, Beth put forth extra effort. In this way, a virtuous cycle of respect is created.

Get Real

Similar to credibility, underlying managers' ability to demonstrate respect must be the fact that they genuinely care about employees. If employees believe that their managers perceive them as "human capital" that exist primarily in the expense column of an organization's income statement, and not as whole people worthy of investment, then few employees will perceive the relationship as fundamentally respectful. An ethic of care may sound "soft," but in reality, caring about and respecting the needs of employees is not an easy thing to do. Because human behavior is not always rational but very often emotional, managers can scarcely be blamed for trying to navigate away from such murky waters as caring. But as consultants, we spend a great deal of time coaching leaders to lean into their discomfort rather than shy away from the complexity of support, collaboration, and caring. Over time, they are able to cultivate an authentic care for their employees.

Take the Employee Perspective

At the best companies, leaders have seen what respect—or a lack thereof—looks like from an employee perspective. They take care to put themselves in the employees' shoes and treat them the way they'd want to be treated. As Rob Burton, the CEO of Hoar Construction, offers, "I can remember one leader who worked here previously who was an outstanding builder. He was an elderly gentleman, and he'd been around for many, many years, and I was a young boy. I went up to ask him one day, 'How do you justify having a company airplane?' He said, 'It's none of your business!' On another occasion, there was an emergency on a job site and I was trying to help. . . . I said, 'Are you guys going to handle this or do you want me to stay involved?' They got mad at me and yelled at me, and said, 'Of course we're going to handle this!' They griped at me. I know what it's like to be an employee in the company. I've done all those jobs and I've been treated in different ways by different people. I know what works and what doesn't. I think I had it in my mind that if I ever got to that position of CEO, it would be different."

Be Mindful That People Bring Their "Whole Being" to Work

Thus, both work-related needs and other, non-work concerns must be addressed. That does not mean that as a manager you need to counsel your employees on family matters. But it does mean that you understand that other aspects of a person's life can impact his or her focus at work, and that you work to actively address that. One of the best companies, Fiat in Brazil, has sign-in boards at the entrances of their plant with traffic light graphics on them. When employees come in to work, they sign their names next to "where they are" that morning; next to the green light if they are present and ready to go, next to the yellow light if they are present but not yet fully engaged, and next to the red light if something is going on for them—they are physically present but not mentally or emotionally present. Managers and human resource professionals review the sign-in boards and pull people from their work stations if they have signed their names in the red area. They check in with them and see if there is something they can do to help them. As you can imagine, it takes a lot of trust for an employee to sign his or her name next to the red light, but more than 80 percent do at least once a year. And if the manager can intervene such that the employee who signed next to the red light is then able to sign next to the yellow or green light, then Fiat has just increased that employee's dedication to his or her work.

Be a Role Model

As a leader, it is imperative that you model the behavior you wish to see in your workplace. Setting the tone so that people—leaders and employees alike—recognize extra effort and understand honest mistakes, collaborate in a spirit of learning and problem solving, and care about the whole person can yield significant dividends for your organization. These are the hallmarks of a respectful work environment, and as a leader, you have a primary role in creating this environment.

RESPECT BEHAVIORAL CHECKLIST

Take a look at the checklist below to see how your leadership behaviors align with how employees experience respect.

Support
- I enable people to get the training and development they need for their career success.
- I give honest and straightforward feedback.
- I know the career "next steps" for each person I supervise, and I create opportunities for them to get relevant experience to meet their career goals.
- I make sure people have the resources they need to do their jobs well.

- I recognize that mistakes are a necessary part of doing business.
- I support people in testing their ideas, even if it has a temporary, negative effect on productivity.
- I talk with people regularly about their growth and development, not just during performance appraisal time.
- I tell people when I think they've done a good job or expended extra effort on a task.

Collaboration

- I ask that my team members gather input from people, in our department and others, before making decisions.
- I create opportunities for us to decide together on the best course of action.
- I follow up with people who have shared ideas and feedback with me.
- I make sure people are involved in the decisions I make that affect them.
- I seek input, suggestions, and ideas from my team.

Caring

- I allow people to take time off when they need to.
- I attend to the collective stress of my workgroup, be it due to personal, time-management, or financial causes.
- I encourage people to balance their work and their personal lives.
- I have an understanding of the benefits the organization offers, and I help people to understand how they can best take advantage of them.
- I know what people in my workgroup enjoy doing outside of work.
- I role model a healthy work-life balance.
- When possible, I attempt to bring the personal skills and passions of people into the workday.

General Mills: Developing Great Managers

Fast Facts:

- Manufacturing—Food Products
- Based in Minneapolis, MN
- Founded in 1866, incorporated in 1928
- Publically traded under the symbol GIS
- 30,000 employees
- List-maker eight times, with additional recognition in the 1984 and 1993 books; recognized internationally fifteen times

At General Mills, the desire to provide learning and development opportunities for employees does not boil down to a set of programs and events. Employees, managers, and the CEO talk readily about its daily importance. SVP of Global Human Resources Mike Davis is currently focused on building great managers, thanks in part to an epiphany. He reflects, "When I got promoted to this job, I wrote four people from my past telling them I had been promoted and thanking them for what they had done. After doing so, I thought, 'That's odd. I wrote four people. Why didn't I write more? I realized I had thirteen bosses, and I wrote four of them notes.' I concluded that those were the great managers who made the difference. I got curious about the whole great management thing, and we did some research with our climate survey. We found unbelievable results that explained everything from discretionary effort to the intention to leave General Mills based upon the strength of someone's manager. So we're really dialing up in this area. We want all managers to be the person that employees talk about when they reflect on their best boss—someone who listens, gets to know people, makes them better, helps them through the tough spots."

It struck us that Davis took his personal reflection on gratitude and transformed it into a professional mandate. This is just one example of how General Mills' leaders have created an environment where professional development becomes an important personal value. It's hard to imagine a place where career development doesn't get stalled by power struggles or the inability to see mistakes as learning opportunities, but General Mills is that place.

When we interviewed them, managers at General Mills shared with us their philosophy about their young employees. One told us, "I've tried to tell people in my group, 'I would love nothing more than to see you advance to the highest levels of this company. I might be reporting to you one day, and I'm okay with that.' I think when people realize that, they will work even harder for you." Another manager told us that he takes cues from how a former manager treats him, "I've noticed a manager three roles ago is still putting in good words for me, and still checking up on me. It's something that's common at General Mills, and something I've started to do as well." And, honoring the place of missteps as a powerful learning tool, CEO Kendall Powell sets the tone. "We've said to people, 'Go for it. You're going to make some mistakes. Try to make small ones. You don't want to learn all your lessons the hard way, but those are spectacular teaching moments.'"

While it is inspiring to see how people's day-to-day support and participation in learning fortifies this aspect of the General Mills culture, leaders have also created programs and practices to further develop their people:

• Individual Development Plans (IDPs) are a cornerstone of development at General Mills. More than just action plans, IDPs come complete with tools and resources. Online tutorials help new employees learn the IDP process and help seasoned professionals identify the best tools given their unique IDP situations. Employees learn how to take into account their personal mix of goals, motivations, career stage, strengths and needs, and job requirements. The tutorial also teaches employees how to evaluate the quality of an IDP, and it provides lessons on avoiding common roadblocks.

- At the General Mills Institute, coursework is updated annually to reflect current development needs and priorities within the organization. Particular emphasis is placed on leadership development, new employee education, and individual and team effectiveness. The General Mills Institute also connects people from across the organization. Senior management plays a role in the teaching of selected coursework, and following coursework, discussion boards help training participants network with each other.

- In order to accelerate individuals' development into key leadership roles, General Mills moves people through a broad path of positions and across a number of divisions and organizations. Cross-functional career growth is encouraged, and to support this, an active and vibrant job rotation program exists in most areas of General Mills. This systematic approach results in thousands of promotions from within and lateral moves each year.

General Mills is a company with a rich heritage, an abundance of recognizable brands, and a palpable sense of pride. Employees are just as proud of their culture as they are of their presence in the community, and learning and development is one aspect they brag about. "What I like most about General Mills is the commitment that it has to its people and learning," says an employee. "There's always a need to update, to learn about what's new. The commitment we have to that is very, very strong."

SC JOHNSON: A FAMILY COMPANY

Fast Facts:

- Manufacturing—Personal and Household Goods
- Based in Racine, WI
- Founded in 1886
- Privately held by the Johnson family
- 12,000 people in 70 countries
- List-maker ten times, with additional recognition in the 1984 and 1993 books; recognized internationally fifty-one times

It is not uncommon among best workplaces to see that the culture created internally has the same characteristics as the identity they create in the marketplace. But perhaps nowhere is that more clear than at SC Johnson. While a fierce competitor in the marketplace, they are also a caring company that places family among their top priorities, and there is a palpable sense of this quality among its employees. More than just a slogan, a sense of family is an anchor of the SC Johnson culture.

The family values begin at the top. The Johnson family are like old friends, both to people within SC Johnson and to the Racine Community. Like their current Chairman and CEO, Fisk Johnson, the family has historically answered only to their first names. Kelly Semrau, Vice President of Global Public Affairs and Communication, says, "Sam was Sam. H.F. was H.F. We're very first-name basis, very informal. Fisk gets uncomfortable if anybody treats him formally. That's the Johnson family. I also knew Sam, and he was an amazing human being. I was meeting with him near his retirement, and he said, 'Kelly, did you know that at this bookstore downtown there is an employee discount? I walked in there the other day and I had on my SC Johnson coat with a logo on it, and they gave me 5 percent off!' I thought to myself, 'Sam, they know who you are! This is downtown Racine.' But, that's the demeanor of the Johnson family—very, very personable, and that carries through the company."

The sense of caring is also apparent in the guiding principles of the company, titled "This We Believe." In a small, blue booklet is a summary of the operating philosophy that has guided the company since 1886. In the first paragraphs, SC Johnson's values directly reference five groups of people—employees, consumers, the general public, neighbors and hosts, and the world community—setting the stage for a far-reaching commitment to earn the trust of all SC Johnson stakeholders.

The first of those stakeholders is employees, many of whom have stories of the caring culture at SC Johnson. One told us, "It really is a family company in that whole sense, from my 7-year-old to my 24-year-old. We've all experienced it. That's the joy, and I love coming to work. The downside is that my kids have very, very high expectations of their employers. Some of them are in situations now where they say, 'Mom, it's not quite like SCJ was. They don't have the same daycare, they don't have this or that.' So, we set an industry standard that I'm very proud of." Another puts it this way, "My manager actually came to me when I was pregnant with the twins, and said, 'What can we do for you?' She saw my needs before I saw my needs. So, as a result, I was given the opportunity over the last few years to work part-time. It really has created a loyalty in me. I believe I am part of this company. I believe I am part of this family, and I will give them my all because of everything they have given to me and my family. I cannot state enough how proud I am to work here, and I am 100 percent committed to this organization."

Leaders not only share these values, they understand how they are intricately linked to the success of the entire organization. Gayle Kosterman, Executive Vice President of Worldwide Human Resources, talks about what she looks for in leaders, "When we hire leaders, we look for people who are strategic and set direction and communicate that. We hire people who get people to want to follow what they're doing, people who are results-oriented, team players, people who value others, and people who are good managers of people." That's a tall order, but SC Johnson's mandate that leaders be caring and authentic, in addition to being results-oriented, is part of who they are.

While leaders are outwardly caring, one doesn't have to look too hard at the programs SC Johnson has to see additional evidence of the company's values:

- SC Johnson's Childcare Learning Center, which opened more than 20 years ago for the exclusive use of employees' kids, is now a 45,000-square-foot facility that cares for about 500 kids every year. The Center has continually expanded over the years to ensure no SC Johnson family ever has to go on a waiting list. The full-service, three-shift Childcare Learning Center is located adjacent to the company's JMBA Recreation & Fitness Center and offers kids access to a wide array of activities and facilities, including a gym, Aquatic Center, and park.
- In 1951, the company purchased the Lighthouse Resort to serve as a vacation spot for SC Johnson's employees and their families. The resort is on Fence Lake in northern Wisconsin and features one-, two-, three-, and four-bedroom cottages as well as duplexes for comfortable family leisure time. Employees, retirees, and their families can enjoy the use of canoes, kayaks, paddleboats, and a pontoon boat for hours of fun in the lake. Program directors offer water ski lessons plus a variety of activities and craft classes for children, teens, and adults. The resort also offers winter leisure options, as it is open year-round.
- SC Johnson's Summer Hours program runs from Memorial Day to Labor Day. During that time, employees who complete their full workweek by noon on Friday can take Friday afternoons off.

While some roles require a set schedule, such as production jobs, many employees, both full- and part-time, are able to work with their teammates and managers to take advantage of this great program that helps them get a head start on the weekend.

Semrau sums up the culture this way, "This company is unique because it truly puts people first and profits come second. Profits are important to us, obviously, but it's very centered around the well-being of the person. The individual is respected here. You feel like you're connected to the top. Fisk takes e-mails and answers questions from everybody. We have an open door policy, so if you walked around today, you would find very few doors closed. It's a culture where you feel taken care of." And it's a culture that has made SC Johnson a bona fide Great Place to Work since we published our first list in 1984.

Case Study

CHAPTER FOUR

FAIRNESS

"Everyone plays by the same rules."

People who succeed here don't expect everybody to be the same. We have such a diversity of people in this company, from different countries, different backgrounds, and different sexual orientations. People don't push themselves to fit into a particular image. If you're going to be successful here, you're going to have to deal with all those different kinds of people without freaking out. The people who can do that, and most of the people in this company can, thrive because they can build the business relationships with people who are wildly different. They not only build business relationships with them, but also enjoy interacting with people who are wildly different from each other.

—GOOGLE EMPLOYEE

Trust requires credibility. Trust requires respect. But if you've read Chapters 2 and 3 and given yourself and your company high marks in the credibility and respect departments, you cannot put a solid "check" next to trust unless you've attended to your employees' experience of fairness. Fairness is the employees' sense that a level playing field exists with regard to decisions that affect them. When fairness is experienced, people feel as though they are treated in an equitable and impartial way, and that their genders, ages, races, and sexual orientations are not factors in assessments of their performance. As elegant as the employee in the opening quote makes it sound, a consistent experience of fairness among employees isn't easy. The third and final building block of trust, fairness is possibly the most difficult to master.

97

To get a sense of just how challenging fairness can be, we need only look at where the bar is set by the best workplaces. Every year, the Great Place to Work Institute calculates benchmarks for each statement on the Trust Index survey we introduced in Chapter One. Across the 100 Best, it is typical that 90 percent of people within each company believe their company is often or almost always a great place to work, and indeed most items on the survey have benchmarks in the high 80s and low 90s. With regard to the fairness statements, benchmarks are much lower, even at the best companies. It is not uncommon to see an average percentage in the high 60- or low 70-percent range for the Fairness statements year to year. While still a healthy majority, it is clear that many employees don't experience fairness consistently, even at the best companies.

So why is it so difficult to create a consistently level playing field? One reason is the very nature of fairness. Perceptions of fairness are driven in large part by the processes leaders use to make decisions. Sometimes those processes are visible, like when Whole Foods Market asks current Team Members to vote new members onto their team after they've been on the job for a few weeks. This transparency serves, in part, as a check against hiring unqualified people. Bringing hiring decisions to a vote also allows current Team Members to be a part of the decision-making process, which increases the collective sense that a decision is fair.

Other times, decision making is not so transparent. Leaders must make tough calls while considering multiple variables, and in some cases, those variables cannot be made known. Even when the variables *can* be made known, the decisions often need to be made quickly and cannot be explained thoroughly beforehand. Thus, no matter what legal obligations, procedural guidelines, or values exist within the company, the perception of fairness boils down to employees' faith in their leaders' ability to make egalitarian decisions whether or not they know why they were made.

Leaders we've coached often feel they are in a catch-22. A leader's trustworthiness depends upon how fair his or her decisions are, but these decisions are not believed to be fair unless the leader is trusted. This is where Chapters 2 and 3 come in. Particularly when you find yourself in conversations about compensation, promotions, and other questions of livelihood, it pays to have built trust in other ways. Fairness rests upon a sense that leaders are reliable (a part of Credibility) and caring (part of Respect). Undoubtedly, it is a complex perception to influence.

As if building fairness wasn't difficult enough, leaders also must recognize that *fair* treatment does not mean *equal* treatment. If it did, the leader's job would be a lot easier. Instead, decisions must be made in ways that acknowledge the individual while honoring the organization as a whole (and the other people within it), which adds complexity to decision making. Consider Robert W. Baird's policy that associates pay health insurance premiums based on their compensation levels, with higher-paid associates paying more than the lower-paid associates. Overall, Baird pays 80 percent on average toward each associate's health care premium, with the range being from 99 percent to 63 percent. The amount varies based on the plan the associate is enrolled in, the coverage level, and the associate's pay band. Baird follows this policy in order to distribute health care costs in a way that acknowledges each associate's ability to pay. While administratively more complex, such a policy improves the sense of fairness.

While complex in some ways, in other ways, balancing caring for the individual and the good of the organization is straightforward. At the 2009 Great Place to Work Conference, Tony Parella, CEO of Shared Technologies, touted a simple philosophy called "Throw the book away!" In his leadership development programs, Parella tells managers that they need to go the extra mile for great employees, no matter what the HR manual says. If employees are taking care of the company, Parella believes the company should take care of them. While an HR manual might be a place to start, it is not where fair treatment ends for valued employees.

As difficult as it is, building a sense of fairness is important to the workplace culture and the ultimate success of the organization. Feeling as though decisions are made fairly provides stability in times of change and uncertainty, even when change is happening so quickly that each decision cannot be explained thoroughly. A sense of fairness can also build camaraderie, since in such an environment, politics and closed-door conversations don't factor into decisions. There is no need to jockey for position (beyond a healthy level of competitiveness) when the work environment is fair. When people are treated fairly, they feel they are equal members of the organization, which leads them to greater commitment and greater effort toward organizational goals. And, lastly, a reputation of being a fair company can help to recruit a broad and diverse labor pool.

Though the Fairness benchmark is comparatively low, there is also a lot of hope on that front. Though still related to the least favorable experiences reported, Fairness benchmarks have improved dramatically since the list began in 1998, and in fact this area has seen more improvement than any other. The largest gain has to do with the absence of politicking and backstabbing, where benchmarks have improved almost 20 points.

More good news: the best companies are doing great things to lead the charge, from disclosing wages company-wide, to introducing formal appeals processes for when disagreements arise. From these examples and more, we see that Fairness can be broken down into three neat categories, and we go through each in this chapter.

EQUITY

Equity reflects the belief that tangible and intangible rewards are distributed in a balanced way. Tangible awards consist of pay and profits, as people need to believe they are compensated fairly in order to have a sense of equity. Less tangibly, they need to feel as though they are equal members of the organization, and that opportunities for recognition come to them as readily as they do other groups of employees. It's important to note that equity is a belief about *process*, not about distribution. Many people would like to be paid more or recognized more often. Equity does not refer to the belief that you are paid or recognized enough. Equity is belief that you are paid and recognized *fairly*.

Pay

Employees at many workplaces believe they are paid fairly for the work they do. That is, employees believe they are compensated reasonably compared to the value they provide to the organization, and the pay they could receive elsewhere for similar work. If the organizations are for-profit, employees at many companies also believe that they receive a fair share of the profits. There are some baseline activities that most companies—whether they are great ones or not—adopt on the pay front to foster a sense of fairness. Many benchmark their salaries against market rates, providing a sense of compensation equity. At most companies, people with more responsibility and authority are paid and incentivized more than those with less responsibility and authority. Yet employees are able to look at their relative effort put in on the job and determine that the distribution of profits is fair.

Baseline HR practices in compensation, such as salary surveys and establishing pay bands, are necessary, but great places to work are not built on baseline activity. Leaders at great companies go above and beyond to ensure that employees feel as though their compensation and profit-sharing are fair. And the ways in which they accomplish this are as different as the organizations themselves.

Sometimes, a greater sense of equity is created simply through communication. Many companies release statements of total compensation, illustrating the total amount spent on an employee in compensation and benefits. Though the statements may clarify how much an employee receives, they may not allay concerns about the *process* by which pay is decided. A different type of communication is necessary to sustain perceptions of equity, and the following provide some examples:

- Whole Foods Market's Wage Disclosure report lists the gross cash compensation (base pay and bonuses) earned by each Team Member—including executives—in the previous calendar year. Any Team Member in the company who wishes to do so may view this report. "Open salary information helps make your compensation system more just, because you have to be prepared to justify what somebody is getting paid," says CEO John Mackey. And he should know. Whole Foods also has a wage cap that limits executives from making more than 19 times a full-time Team Member's salary.

- At T-Mobile, managers are empowered to communicate well about compensation. Leaders take a Comp 101 course delivered by the company's compensation team. The course details T-Mobile's philosophy and practices around pay, so there is consistency across T-Mobile when explaining performance and compensation. It also ensures that leaders are making fair and effective decisions regarding pay. The company also has an online training course in compensation for all employees, along with special training programs for new hires and newly promoted managers.

- American Fidelity Assurance relies upon its own employees to communicate, in large part because its employees are the ones making the compensation decisions! American Fidelity's Compensation Review Team (CRT) consists of members from all divisions in the company. Human Resources staff members serve as the project coordinators and administrators of compensation while the CRT makes decisions and manages the program. Another unique characteristic of the CRT is that most members have become experts on American Fidelity's compensation approach and strategy and take the lead in educating fellow colleagues in their respective divisions. When signing up to be a member, no individual on the team had a compensation background, nor did anyone know that years later they would become expert communicators about compensation. Thus, American Fidelity not only increases the sense of equity by enabling its colleagues to communicate about pay, it creates a more equitable process at the outset by involving employees in the process.

Many of the best companies also have egalitarian profit-sharing programs that award bonuses to employees at all levels of the organization. In most companies, bonuses are reserved for those at the highest levels in the organization, since they are the ones who have the most responsibility for profit and loss. However, the best have found a way to make bonuses both attainable and relevant for all employees. For instance, Valero Energy Corporation, which owns and operates refineries and retail gas stations, recognizes employees at all levels—in both retail and non-retail—with cash bonuses. Bonuses for retail store managers and assistant managers are based on store performance, and bonuses for employees who work in the stores and gas stations are based on customer service. Executives receive bonuses only when all employees receive bonuses. By tying bonuses to outcomes that employees have control over, Valero leaders also send a message about what each employee needs to do to succeed. This, in turn, reinforces a sense of fairness in the share of the profits received.

Perhaps the ultimate signal of fair pay and profit-sharing comes with employee stock ownership. Several companies on the list over the years espouse employee ownership, including Publix Super Markets, Boston Consulting Group, and TDIndustries, to name just a few. Not only does employee ownership provide fairness in profit-sharing by design, but it also creates a sense of responsibility on the part of employees in carrying out their day-to-day work. CH2M HILL is an employee-owned engineering and construction firm based in Denver, Colorado. Margaret McLean, Chief Legal Officer at CH2M HILL, says, "The fact that we are employee-owned plays a huge part in how we think about the company and what we do. At the end of the day, you are working for those you work with. They own this company. I know in conversations with my internal clients and my team, it's always about the fact that we are protecting our nest egg, we are protecting our children's college fund, and we are protecting our legacy. It changes the dialogue."

Membership

While pay is one signal of worth in an organization, feeling like an equal member is quite another. Membership is more intangible than pay, but just as powerful. Equity in membership is the belief that all employees, regardless of their position, are treated in a way that conveys their full value and worth to the organization. When companies get this right, even people in lower-status positions—whether by pay or hierarchy— are engaged in the organization and its activities to the same degree as people in higher-status positions. Like most aspects of fairness, much of membership equity is behavior-driven, not policy-driven. It is evident in the way managers speak to others, and in the way they make decisions and communicate them. Having said that, membership is also signaled to employees through programs and practices.

Programs that recognize and cater to the needs of individual groups of employees are common among the best companies. Such programs can create a sense of full membership in the organization by showing employees that their needs matter, even if they aren't the needs of everyone. Some programs are tailored to employees working evening or overnight shifts, while other programs accommodate new parents, and still others address the needs of employees whose needs may simply deviate from the norm:

- Many Four Seasons Hotels have extended hours in Human Resources to accommodate the various schedules of their staff. HR staff are available on Saturdays, and for evening hours until 8:00 P.M. They also hold 2:00 A.M. "benefits breakfasts" for overnight staff to ensure that all employees receive the information they need.
- Boston Consulting Group (BCG), a strategic and managerial consultancy, hires people with a variety of backgrounds, and they also understand the importance of providing skills foundational to success regardless of those backgrounds. Twice a year BCG holds the Business Essentials Program (BEP), an intensive, two-week off-site training session for new BCG hires who do not hold MBA degrees and for associates promoted to consultant who will not be pursuing an MBA in the near future. The program is designed to aid in the early success of non-MBA hires by providing grounding and comfort in the basic principles of business, extending views of business beyond narrowly focused experiences, and developing employees' command of analytical skills and tools. Like employees at all levels, professionals, managers, and leaders benefit when their unique needs are recognized and met, and in many cases, the sense of equity spills over into positive relationships with the coworkers and clients.

Many recognition programs follow the same pattern of paying deliberate attention to all groups of people whose contributions make a difference, and devising meaningful ways of recognizing them. Note that in the previous chapter, we talked about building respect by recognizing employees. Here, we mean to convey that you can build a sense of fairness by giving everyone an equal chance at being recognized, no matter their position. For instance, Nugget Market has an annual Bag-Off contest, where courtesy clerks compete for the title of the fastest bagger. But Nugget also uses the opportunity as a way to recognize everyone in the store, no matter their role. As the stores gear up for the annual Bag-Off contests, Nugget simultaneously holds the Spirit Competition. Using costumes, face paint, songs, and cheers, stores compete not only to see who has the best baggers but also to see which store has the most spirit. The winner receives the coveted Spirit Trophy, as well as bragging rights for the next year.

Peer recognition programs are often overlooked, but can be a great way to help employees feel more like full members of the organization. Not only are employees given autonomy to recognize employees they feel are succeeding, but peer recognition is also a leveling mechanism whereby everyone who comes into contact with another employee is eligible for recognition. At Erickson Retirement Communities, a community management company based in Baltimore, Maryland, "Best of the Best" awards are presented to one exempt and one non-exempt employee working in the corporate offices and at each community. To be considered for this award, nominees must have received accolades from fellow employees, residents, or visitors for embracing the company culture and values and making Erickson a great place to work, live, and visit. Winners are announced during executive team visits to each community so executives are on hand to personally present the recipient with a plaque and words of congratulations in the presence of supervisors and peers. Recipients also receive a monetary award as well as other gifts that are selected by the leaders of their department or community.

IMPARTIALITY

Whereas equity is the belief in a fair process and equal membership in the organization, impartiality is the belief in evenhanded decision making. A belief in impartiality is faith that management avoids favoritism and actively promotes the fair assessment of people for positions and work assignments. In other words, people believe in your ability to make decisions on the basis of the right things—not politics, friendship, or personal gain. Of all three components of Fairness, this is the one that is the most difficult, as borne out by the low benchmarks and our personal experience coaching managers.

There are several reasons why impartiality is so challenging for leaders. It is difficult to show employees you care without being seen as playing favorites, and it is hard to make important decisions without someone thinking he or she has a better idea, particularly if it means that someone was not chosen for promotion or recognition. In our experience, it is when managers think too much about striking this balance that they mess it up! The right thing to do is often the most caring thing. And the tough decision is often best for everyone involved if it is made fairly.

Being able to communicate resolves many impartiality concerns, and managers are more likely to communicate when they can stand firmly behind their decision. We often suggest that managers make the decision they feel is right, expect fallout, and plan to communicate. Paradoxically, if managers try to make a decision that won't create fallout, or if they don't plan their communication, they are more likely to make a decision that is unfair in some way. Here again, a company's guiding values are a beacon for both the manager and the organization. Values help a manager to make decisions in line with the organization's philosophy, and decisions across the organization then have a consistency that is the hallmark of impartiality.

Several companies incorporate fairness into their value systems, which creates impartiality by setting a standard for decision making. Leaders at best companies also take steps to ensure that the message is heard and understood by managers at all levels:

- TDIndustries' mission statement is: "We are committed to providing outstanding career opportunities by exceeding our customers' expectations through continuous aggressive improvement." Career opportunities are considered part of their mission. Moreover, TDIndustries leaders are held to a standard of "servant leadership"— a philosophy that teaches managers to serve the people who work for them, and not the other way around. Both principles set the tone for fair decision making on the part of managers.

- CH2M HILL employees at all levels abide by the "Little Yellow Book," written by a beloved cofounder and former chairman. One of the thoughts in the book is: "Supervisors so often say, 'I want you to do this' or 'I want you to do that.' Better to say, 'It will work best if you do this' or 'To conform to the firm's policies, please do that.' We do things because it is good for the company, not because of an individual's desires." Leaders take these words to heart! In our interviews with CH2M HILL's senior executives, many of them showed up with copies of the "Little Yellow Book" in their pockets.

- One of Bright Horizon's "Mission in Motion" elements is *"Play It Forward:* Help to develop a new generation of leaders." And they do. Their Succession Planning Program identifies future leaders and implements individual development plans, which serves to support key contributors and enable them to be promoted within the organization. Managers evaluate their teams and rank their performance and potential based on objective measures, and managers are expected to give feedback and engage in honest dialog with employees to guide their career progression.

Why are values so important when it comes to impartiality? No program, practice, or initiative can force good behavior on the part of managers; managers are given the authority to make decisions, and leaders and employees must afford them some degree of latitude in making the appropriate ones. A solid set of values, the presence of strong role models, and clear communications about the necessity of fairness in decision making are more powerful than policy and procedure. This is not to say policies and programs meant to bolster fairness aren't important, but it is the execution of policy and the outcomes of programs that send the real message of impartiality.

Take the case of promotions. When promotions are made fairly, a philosophy of promotion from within can create perceptions of impartiality. If the person being promoted is a high-performing and well-respected peer, employees are more likely to see the promotion as deserved. Companies can facilitate the process by being sure they are aware of people who desire a promotion and supporting those people in gaining the requisite skills. Promotion from within has allowed hundreds of thousands of people at Publix Super Markets to reach their career goals by starting in entry-level positions and receiving training on the job throughout their careers. Publix's management Registration of Interest (ROI) process allows associates to formally express their interest in being promoted to a retail management position. The ROI process enables Publix to understand the career aspirations of associates and help them prepare for their desired roles. Employees in organizations where similar processes are in place understand that promotions are made after considering the applications of those who expressed interest, and closing skill gaps as needed. People understand the philosophy of impartiality at Publix not because this program is on the books, but because it is executed and they see results.

In other companies, employees themselves play a large part in determining who should be promoted or recognized. When employees recommend their peers, the decision is better accepted by fellow employees because the people who had the most opportunity to observe performance also made the call as to whether that performance merits reward or promotion. Members of the President's Club at Umpqua Bank work in many different areas of the bank. They are nominated by associates for embracing the company's core values and culture, and then must receive a 75 percent approval rating from the current members of the club (around 100 people). President's Club members become a conduit for communication between associates and executives, providing an avenue of communication for concerns, and so associates feel a greater sense of impartiality if they get to nominate them.

As you can see, impartiality boils down to decision making. While some decisions are quite visible and consequential for a manager's material success, many are not. But all decisions that involve employees, whether formally reviewed by others or not, have an impact upon impressions of impartiality. Whether through your creation of formal programs, company values, or your own role modeling, your job as a leader includes giving guidance to others in making fair and impartial decisions.

JUSTICE

A strong sense of justice, like equity and impartiality, is not easy to obtain in a work environment. It builds on the belief that leaders are credible, and that their actions match their words. Employees experiencing a just work environment believe that management promotes inclusive behavior, avoids discrimination, and is committed to ensuring fair appeals. While many programs exist to forward a sense of justice, such as diversity training and grievance procedures, once again this perception sits more squarely upon the behavior of individual managers. Companies that are successful in creating a sense of justice hold managers responsible for treating people without bias. Additionally, leaders in these best companies want to hear from people who feel as though they've been treated unfairly, and will consider their appeals carefully.

Treatment

Justice is grounded in ensuring fair treatment of all employees, regardless of personal characteristics such as race, age, gender, ability, and sexual orientation. Over the last 50 years, we've seen companies focus more and more on diversity. But it's only been in recent years that we've seen a shift from "meeting legal requirements" to fostering a culture of inclusion, and list-making companies have been leaders in doing so.

From our perspective, the shift looks like this: where companies used to focus solely on getting numerical counts of employees to acceptable levels through hiring and recruiting, leaders now use those numbers as a way to measure the *outcome* of their efforts to build an inclusive culture. The counts are still monitored and actions are still taken to improve representativeness, but in the best companies, the focus is on finding ways to engage the perspectives and talents of people of all backgrounds. It's more than just reacting to the numbers; inclusiveness is a part of their values, their strategies, and the expectations they have for people across the organization.

The most common programs or practices we see in companies to address this issue are programs that support diverse groups of employees, target recruiting to under-represented groups, and maintain a strategic focus on diversity.

- As part of taking care of their diverse associates, Marriott International launched a suite of company-sponsored language-training programs and self-paced language-development resources to help their workforce increase their opportunities for career and personal development. As part of this program, in 2009 Marriott expanded their Rosetta Stone® language courses through the company's myLearning website. With 30 languages to choose from, the courses enhance language proficiency by improving communication among associates and customers. More than 5,200 associates are currently active in the program.
- With hopes to generate leads for more diversity among new hires, General Mills, a leading manufacturer and marketer in the

consumer food products industry, adopted Bring a Friend Night. Members of the company's various Employee Networks, which are internal support systems to help women and minorities advance, are invited to bring their friends and families to an open house. Employees are awarded $3,000 for guests who are hired as a result of attending these events. Events have been standing-room only, with upwards of 260 guests in attendance.

- At Perkins Coie, a Seattle-based law firm with over a dozen offices worldwide, lawyers at all levels of practice and representing almost every U.S. office serve on the firm-wide Strategic Diversity Committee. The work of this committee originally began in 1988, and has provided a forum for discussion and implementation of a variety of programs and policies affecting women and other diverse lawyers. The Diversity Strategic Committee is charged with developing the firm-wide diversity strategy, setting goals to guide the implementation of existing programs, and creating new initiatives. They also provide input to the Executive and Management Committees about the direct and indirect effects that firm initiatives have on workplace diversity. The group is composed of fourteen partners, four of-counsel attorneys, five associates, and five administrative staff members, including the Chief Operating Officer, Chief Diversity Officer, Chief Marketing Officer, and the Chief Personnel Officer. The firm's Managing Partner is also a member of the Strategic Diversity Committee.

- PricewaterhouseCoopers LLP (PwC), a global professional services firm, reaches out to minority college freshmen and sophomores through a program called "eXplore." eXplore is a day-long interactive curriculum aimed at developing teamwork, strategic thinking, creativity, problem solving, and leadership skills. It's a fun and educational day that includes social networking, a group dinner, and raffle prizes. It allows small groups of students (no more than 40) to ask questions and get a feel for what a career at PwC is like. Students who show interest are then considered for talent development programs and internships. eXplore supports the firm's efforts to attract diverse candidates and opens the door to candidates who might not otherwise think of a career in a Big Four accounting firm.

While many companies have taken steps to level the playing field for people of all genders, races, ages, ability levels, and sexual orientations, the programs and practices in the best companies are among the most cutting edge. Additionally, programs in these companies often target the subtleties of fair treatment with impressive precision. Take TDIndustries, a company with many Spanish-speaking employees. While many companies offer English classes for their non-English speakers, TDIndustries aims to resolve the real issue at hand: communication. At TD, you'll also find Spanish classes being taken by English-speaking employees. Consider the message this sends about fair treatment. No group is singled out. No group is seen as the one needing to assimilate. Rather, it benefits everyone if employees can communicate with one another. A common language, be it Spanish or English, makes that possible.

Another unique program that gracefully addresses more deeply seated issues of fair treatment is found at W. L. Gore. Leaders at Gore listen to an often forgotten group when it comes to conversations about diversity. In addition to more traditional diversity networks such as African-American, Asian, Latino-Hispanic, gay and lesbian, and women's networks, they have also formed a White Men Supporting Diversity network. This group was initiated by men who wanted to find a way to remain a part of the diversity conversation, supporting other associates and the culture. Again, note the message this sends. It's not about groups that are only open to people of color or women; it is about addressing the diversity needs and interests of all employees, including those of white men.

Appeals

The other aspect of justice involves employees' confidence that they can appeal any decision, and that they will get a fair hearing if they do. Some companies handle all concerns with an open door policy that encourages employees to approach any manager, at any time, with any issue. While an ideal situation, the open door policy only works if it is firmly ingrained in the organization, if it has often been tested by history, and if it is supported by stories of employees successfully challenging the status quo by doing nothing more than approaching a manager and voicing a concern. It's unlikely to successfully create such an environment from scratch, but not impossible. Usually, successful open door policies begin with some sort of formal process, even a basic one that encourages employees to involve the HR staff. Over time, and consistently feeling a sense of justice and fairness, employees begin to feel fully supported in raising a concern.

Often, the mere presence of a clear and publicized policy for handling grievances or concerns improves employees' sense of justice. We've worked with companies that have seen dramatic improvements in employee perceptions simply by instating a grievance process. If leaders and managers support the grievance process, encourage its use, and respond appropriately to concerns involving them, employees will feel a sense of justice when it comes to appeals. However, there are several other ways to make employees feel more comfortable about making an appeal. Large companies, in particular, often find that a more structured approach is needed.

With 60,000 employees worldwide, American Express is one of those companies. The Office of the Ombudsperson is a confidential and neutral resource where employees can seek guidance without fear of retribution, and with confidence that their concerns will remain "off the record." The Office consists of ombudspersons around the world who listen to, coach, and assist employees. It is the employee who then decides on the best course of action that works for him or her. For example, an ombudsperson at American Express can

- Provide employees with coaching on how best to approach their leader or use other formal channels within the company to resolve their issue;
- Help employees pass on information to their leader or other individuals while protecting their identity; and
- Identify alternative options when employees have already approached their leader with an issue but reached no resolution.

To promote an inclusive employee offering, ombudspersons are well versed in the company's diversity initiatives—in the United States, the ombudsperson is a member of the Diversity Council. In addition, ombudspersons meet periodically with members of senior management to identify trends and opportunities for systemic improvement. Thus, American Express provides outreach to employees who are in need of support in raising a concern, but they also gather information so as to correct ongoing problems and more permanently resolve the issues at hand.

Many other companies, large and small, include peer review processes in their grievance procedures. Not only does this provide the employee with a group of peers who may better understand the employee's concerns, but also it provides checks and balances that lead to greater perceptions of fairness. In other words, peer review programs provide a way for leaders to demonstrate their commitment to fairness to multiple employees at once, spreading the word about what to expect when others have raised concerns. Granite Construction has an Employee Dispute Resolution Program (EDRP) with four options an employee can use to challenge or appeal a decision. Option 1 is an open door policy that allows an employee to talk to his or her immediate supervisor or to a higher level of management without fear of retaliation. Option 2 is a dispute resolution conference. This is a conference with a team of three or four peers and managers who are not involved in the situation and can be fair and unbiased to all parties involved. Option 3 is mediation through the American Arbitration Association (AAA). Option 4 is arbitration through the AAA. If an employee requests representation by an attorney, Granite will pay up to $2,500 for their legal fees during the process. While most of the employee disputes at the company are resolved through the employee helpline, in consultation with the Human Resources Department, or through Option 1, the ability to participate in one these options undoubtedly increases employees' sense of justice.

LEADER IMPERATIVES

We often tell leaders that fairness cannot be created in a vacuum. More than any other dimension, fairness improves if efforts are also made to strengthen the other anchors of trust. A first step may be to take action to build credibility and respect in order to buoy your employees' perception of fairness. The other imperatives to consider follow.

Keep Fairness Top of Mind
Determine where fair treatment falls in your company's statement of values, and then publicize and remind people of the imperative to treat others with impartiality and justice, no matter their position in the organization. QUALCOMM believes that each of their employees contributes to industry leadership, and each year, teams are selected from each division to represent these contributions in the QUALCOMM Annual Report About People. Each report features employees from around the world—whether they're representing a team or function,

or sharing their thoughts about the company. This internal publication showcases how employees and teams contributed to QUALCOMM's success over the past year and highlights the unique company culture. In the best companies, even their internal communications send signals that people matter, regardless of position. As you assess your workplace, ask if your messaging makes people feel as though they are equal members, reminds people that everyone has a contribution to make, and indirectly encourages managers to take fairness into consideration when making decisions.

Take a Zero-Tolerance Attitude Toward Unfairness

Hold managers accountable when it comes to unfair treatment. Steven Stanbrook, COO of International Markets at SC Johnson, says that adopting such an attitude is fundamental to a strong culture. "I think that is what makes the values real. If we didn't address mistakes, the values would literally mean nothing because in order to make a statement about what we will do, it's also making a statement about what we will not tolerate. I think if you don't fulfill that latter part of the values statement, they truly are words on a page. I try to encourage people to be empathetic, and to see the situation from the other person's point of view. But, if it still doesn't reflect good judgment, there will be consequences." If leaders don't educate managers about the importance of fair decision making, and reprimand those who don't act justly, employees cannot trust that they will be treated with equity, impartiality, and respect.

Send Strong Messages

Decisions about promotions and titles, and the procedures underlying them, send a message about fairness. As mentioned above, American Express has appointed a team of people who are there to help employees get their concerns addressed in a just way. But strong messages can also be sent in the way a leader interacts with his or her people. A manager at Wegmans talked with us about his philosophy of leadership this way: "We do have titles, but none of us like to use them because it's not fair to our employees. When they need something from us, it doesn't matter who it is, we have to produce for them. Period. At any level." Consider how to send a loud and clear message about fairness no matter your influence level. Even if promotions and procedures are out of your realm of responsibility, your personal philosophies speak volumes about how you believe employees should be treated.

Get Involved

When top leaders are involved in decision making, even as a final review, both managers and employees know that fairness is expected. At QuikTrip, a Tulsa-based convenience store, the president-CEO and the twelve VPs review each employee's pay. This takes approximately four days to complete. QuikTrip conducts this review for all positions, from mail clerk to vice-president. Pay is given a huge time commitment from everyone at the top to ensure that it is fair and consistent. Leaders must take care to make sure reviews are seen as components of partnerships rather than of micromanagement. But, with something as precarious as employees' perceptions of fairness on the line, the additional time and attention are warranted.

Once you send these messages, your managers are more likely to take action.

FAIRNESS BEHAVIORAL CHECKLIST

A behavioral checklist to create an environment with equity, impartiality, and justice includes

Equity

- I communicate about the distribution of profits made by the organization.
- I ensure that people understand the factors influencing their pay.
- I recognize people when they do a good job, regardless of their positions or tenure in my workgroup.
- I treat people with respect no matter their positions in my workgroup or the organization.
- I work to ensure fair pay for the people in my workgroup.

Impartiality

- I disentangle myself from political motivations when I find myself involved.
- I ensure that people are well positioned for promotion when they are ready for advancement.
- I let people know what's needed to seek promotions within my department.
- I make an effort to build meaningful relationships with each of my direct reports.
- I take care not to spread rumors.
- I try to act in the best interest of everyone involved in my work life: my organization, my people, and myself.
- I try to avoid giving any employees preferential treatment.
- When people get promotions in my department, I communicate to others their qualifications for the new roles.

Justice

- I give people opportunities and treat people with respect regardless of their ages.
- I give people opportunities and treat people with respect regardless of their genders.

- I give people opportunities and treat people with respect regardless of their races.
- I give people opportunities and treat people with respect regardless of their sexual orientations.
- I make sure people are aware of how to appeal decisions made by their leaders.
- I respond supportively to people who approach me with concerns about mistreatment.

Scripps Health: All for One and One for All

Fast Facts:
- Health Care System Including Five Hospitals, Ambulatory Care Clinics, and Home Health Services
- Based in San Diego, CA
- Founded in 1924 by Ellen Browning Scripps
- Nonprofit
- 13,200 employees in 29 locations
- List-maker since 2008

Scripps Health employees enjoy several aspects of their work. They take pride in the care they give their patients. They have strong leaders who have built upon Scripps' legacy to create a first-class health care organization. They have a fun and family-oriented work environment. And they enjoy generous and targeted benefits. But what is most striking about Scripps is the clear sense that everyone matters. When you talk to employees, they say that they are "all in this together." This sense of team doesn't happen by accident, and it is no small feat given that Scripps' locations are very diverse, both in their histories and in the communities they serve. To achieve this team environment, leaders set the tone by sending strong messages and deliberately creating programs and benefits that reach everyone. Everywhere you look at Scripps, you see a level playing field, reinforced through word and deed.

SVP of Innovation, Human Resources, and Performance Management, Vic Buzachero, conducts focus groups on a yearly basis to understand the needs of people and to tailor programs to meet them. When designing their employee incentive program, Vic looked to employees to help him create a program that was simple and meaningful. "Employees really defined what they thought they could control and how it should work. We use that information and then communicate: 'Here's what you said you wanted, here's what we put together.' And we made it simpler than most employee incentive programs." Today, through the Success Shares program, if certain goals are met, Scripps awards several million dollars across all employees working over 1,086 hours that calendar year. No one employee can do it alone. The payback signals fairness in the way profits are distributed, and the goals themselves encourage cooperation. At the end of the day, people feel as though they are all important to the success of Scripps, and they all get to share in that success.

Other programs that Scripps uses to foster their culture of equity and full membership include the following:

- Scripps' New Employee Orientation helps each new employee understand how his or her work contributes to Scripps' strategic goals, no matter the location or role. This full-day program underscores the mission, the vision, the expectation for quality care on the part of employees, and the provision of support and development on the part of the organization. From their very first day, people gain an understanding of their important part in delivering quality health care.
- Many benefits and programs are designed to serve all employees. Each year, each employee participates in at least one learning program, and tuition reimbursement programs are available to everyone. Even non-clinical staff can receive money toward a clinical degree, and employees with limited English proficiency can participate through Scripps' Essential Career Pathways program.
- Efforts also target the unique needs of particular groups. Retirees are an example of a group often forgotten by companies once they leave, but not at Scripps! Scripps retirees receive special communications, wellness benefits, and invitations to celebrations as ways to recognize their service. Another group Scripps targets are entry-level employees, who receive subsidies on their

health care benefits as a way to help them obtain a fair wage in the expensive San Diego marketplace.

Not only are Scripps programs evidence of their commitment to the involvement of every employee, the philosophies of their managers send the message loud and clear. As one nurse manager puts it, "I think that whether you are in ancillary service or nursing or any department, the expectation of leadership at Scripps is that the leader can do any job that the employees can do. Yes, there is a hierarchy, but really there isn't. There is a team atmosphere that is expected. Leaders are not brought into that leadership role, or typically shouldn't be brought into that role, if they don't foster that team environment. The bottom line is, I am a nurse and a manager. But the staff bedside nurse is the expert."

The payoff of these programs and philosophies is seen in the commitment and cooperation of Scripps employees, and in excellent patient care. One employee sums it up: "We are all here to make sure that patients get good care. Everybody sticks together and helps each other. I can call engineering, I can call housekeeping, I can call the floors of the ICU, anybody. And they are going to help me get what I need to get accomplished in a day's time, and without even needing to think about it."

Case Study

CH2M HILL: Ownership as a Way of Life

Fast Facts:

- Professional Services—Consulting, Design, Design-Build, Operations, and Program Management
- Based in Englewood, CO
- Founded in 1946
- Privately held and employee-owned
- 23,500 employees in more than 170 offices around the world
- List-maker in 2003, 2006, 2008, and 2009

CH2M HILL is an employee-owned engineering and construction firm based in Denver, Colorado. Thus, their "act-like-an-owner" philosophy is put directly into practice through CH2M HILL's employee ownership program. It is inspiring for employees to know that personal performance can contribute to improved investment returns, whether they actually participate as shareholders or not. Regardless of their personal ownership statuses, all employees see themselves as working for a close-knit community of owners rather than a distant group of public stockholders or an exclusive group of privileged partners. What does "acting like an owner" mean? At CH2M HILL, it means sharing expertise, keeping the well-being of the company and its people in mind when making decisions, and walking the talk when it comes to company philosophies.

At CH2M HILL employees resoundingly reference the sharing of knowledge and expertise across the organization as a hallmark of the culture. As one employee said, "I always like to tell people that I very rarely work alone because the teaming that you do, whether or not it's within your own department or cross-functionally or cross-business group, it's always a team of people that are on a project that you're working on. It's hardly ever something that you're doing on your own." Bob Card, President of the Facilities and Infrastructure Division, goes even further with the importance of sharing expertise. "I've always referred to us as having empowered autonomy. We wouldn't be telling you the truth if we said we control our divisions. We lead them. The true organization here is based on talent. We can publish all the charts you want, but the lines will always flow to where the answers are."

Employees also comment upon how private ownership allows them to take a long-term view. "One thing you can say at an employee-held company," said an employee, "is that it really does give us the luxury of taking a longer-term view of what's good for the business and there's never any real pressure to meet a short-term number or even a mid-term number. I work in an area where I'm responsible for evaluating risk profiles on projects. If a project looks very attractive financially, but has a risk profile that puts the company in potential financial jeopardy, we are very quick to say no. We will pick and choose what it is we want to work on based on the long-term goals of the company versus somebody trying to hit a sales number or margin target."

Acting like an owner means acting in accordance with the philosophies in the "Little Yellow Book." Written and illustrated by cofounder and former chairman Jim Howland, the book is carried around by many executives who are quick to reference their favorite passages. Keeping these philosophies top of mind is a solid reminder to employees of their obligations. One employee told us, "In acquiring other companies, we go through the risk assessment and take a look at what their status is. My manager in one of our integration meetings said, 'At the end of the day, would you want to see this on the front page of the newspaper?' That's a direct quote from the 'Little Yellow Book.' That's how we need to look at all situations. That's how we start our training and integration. Hearing managers refer to passages is proof that our values are alive."

Of course, the employee ownership aspect of CH2M HILL is also unique, even among the best companies to work for. Though they do not disclose detailed information about the number of employees participating, all stock is held by employees. Leaders are quick to point out that while ownership itself is positive, it's the way that employee ownership allows them to operate that makes the difference. Leaders and employees alike act like owners at CH2M HILL, but more important, they act like owners of a great workplace. They take personal responsibility for sharing information with each other, making decisions that are best for the business in the long term, and living the organization's values.

"Because we are employee-owned, we chart our own course and make the business decisions that are best for our employees and clients," said Lee McIntire, CH2M HILL Chairman and CEO. "We have over 23,000 employees who we trust to do the right thing, and our employee owners hold us accountable to do the same. There are no analysts. No short-selling. No one on Wall Street who runs this company—it's actually us."

CHAPTER FIVE

PRIDE

"I contribute to something really meaningful."

This company takes pride in empowering its people to a point where they do not feel like they are just "doing a job," they are actually playing a pivotal role in the company.
—WEGMANS EMPLOYEE

I t's clear that employees are in a relationship with their management (and if it wasn't clear before picking up this book, Chapters 2, 3, and 4 should have convinced you), but just as significantly, employees are in a relationship with their *jobs*. In fact, this is the relationship that receives the most attention from managers and human resource professionals; most leaders focus squarely on trying to document, measure, improve, and monitor an employee's engagement with his or her job, and human resource professionals focus on related issues such as engagement, job enrichment, and competencies. So it only makes sense that we consider what aspects of this relationship are core to an *employee's* experience of a workplace being "great."

The best way to talk about this relationship is to describe the underlying sense of pride that employees have in their job, team, and company. When we ask employees in great workplaces to describe what it is like to work there, they begin to smile and talk about how they are excited to get to work, and then, at the end of a day, are surprised to discover that the day has already disappeared. They are fully wrapped up in their

127

work, and time just seems to fly by. They share their belief that what they do matters in the organization—that their team or the organization would be less successful if it weren't for their efforts. They also talk about the joy they have in seeing the output of their team's work, and share a real sense of appreciation for the company—its brand, its products and services, and its standing in the community. They say things like "I want to retire from here" and "I *get* to come to work here—what a privilege," and "We have amazing products."

For many organizations that use our employee survey, Pride tends to be the most positive of the five dimensions. This is little surprise, really. The job is the preeminent aspect of our work experience, and we are not likely to stay for very long if the job itself doesn't hold much interest for us, is too challenging, or is not challenging enough. And while an employee might not have great trust in her manager or the executive team, she can at least have pride in her team's accomplishments or the products or services that her company produces.

Pride in your work is elemental, but it also makes a strong impact on an organization's success. Employees who are proud of their company and its products and services make great brand ambassadors; indeed, for many organizations, their brand promise is based on the service, reliability, or skill of the organization's people. Employees who take pride in their job and see their work as having special meaning are more willing to give more than what is required, and are more committed to their department and company's goals. In short, having a strong sense of pride impacts an employee's discretionary effort.

As we mentioned in the first chapter, the best companies, on average, have half the voluntary turnover of their industry peers. People want to stay with great employers, and when the costs associated with finding a replacement can creep up to two or more times the amount of that person's salary, it pays to create a work environment where people want to stay. So when employees want to stay for a long time, when they have meaningful work, and when they are proud of their accomplishments in their team and association with the enterprise, then you have a significantly more engaged and productive workforce.

You may already know how important pride is to the successful operation of your business. You may try to hire people who take pride in their work, and whose values will match up with those of the company. What you may not know is how to enhance pride while fulfilling your leadership role. As we've discussed, you have a very direct role and responsibility for developing a high-trust work environment. Pride is somewhat different. As a manager or leader, you have a less direct impact on an employee's experience of pride. But make no mistake about it— these relationships are interdependent (as is the relationship we'll cover in the next chapter, the relationship of employees with one another). Your efforts at building trust also support pride. And as for building pride itself, there are some concrete actions that you can take directly to foster the sense of pride employees take in their job, in their team, and in their company. We'll go through these areas one at a time.

PERSONAL PRIDE IN ONE'S JOB

Personal pride refers to how employees view their individual contributions to the organization. We believe that most employees in most organizations *want* to make a contribution and take pride in their work most of the time. They want to believe that they make a difference at the organization itself. And they want to believe their work has special meaning to the world outside of the organization. They want to feel as though they are making a positive impact in the world.

Making a Difference
When employees believe that their efforts make a difference, they feel that their work has an impact on the organization, and that their personal

presence in the workplace (independent of their job description) also makes a difference, we find that people take pride in their work and the accomplishment of organizational goals and functions.

Making a difference operates on two levels. The first: employees believe they have an impact in their actual job or sphere of responsibility. As a Microsoft employee put it, "Microsoft is a really big company. When people think about working at Microsoft they don't feel that they are going to have a lot of influence. The reality is, if you want to have a lot of influence, if you want to have a large project, that's very possible." The other level: employees believe they themselves actually matter in the organization, beyond their narrow function. As employees at Camden, the community managers, offered of their leadership, "They figure everyone here is an important asset. It's not just [the] work, but you feel like you are really a part of Camden and that every person really matters."

In both cases, employees are describing a sense of personal authority at work. What this means is that they are empowered to take things on, make decisions, and see the results of their work. They feel like they can make a difference because they are able to actually see the difference they make. Camden prides itself in creating a community for those who live at their properties, so it was in keeping with the Camden philosophy that one employee came up with the idea to plan a pet expo. When describing this example of positive influence, the employee said, "The next thing you know, I am in charge of this regional event and they are giving me cards and telling me to order supplies and get volunteers from other communities, and I was just so empowered and it was just such a proud moment that they trusted me and I felt trusted, and it was such a fun, awesome event." And this employee isn't in the marketing department!

When employees have this sense of personal authority, they usually have the freedom to move beyond a specific job role or task; employees can exercise some degree of creativity and innovation, and leave their own marks. There is an appropriate amount of both challenge and support, such that an employee experiences a sense of competence with the work. Significantly, they are validated for their efforts. As a leader, you can support people in feeling like they matter by providing them the room and autonomy to "take the ball and run with it," providing positive and constructive feedback along the way, and recognizing such efforts when they happen.

Leaders can also look at an organization's values and structure—do conditions exist that support employees' sense of making a difference? Google's core values, for instance, are oriented toward impressing upon every employee the importance of his or her role in the larger picture. They believe that their people truly do matter, not only to Google, but to the world. Another Google condition: they have a relatively flat organizational structure that promotes a comfortable environment to share ideas. This structure enables all members to directly participate in the implementation of numerous products and policies, instilling a sense of empowerment among employees. This kind of purposeful structuring of the work environment helps employees say, "I can do this!" Employees feel like their work and personal contributions matter to Google.

Meaningful Work

The other aspect of personal pride is employees' belief that their work has special meaning. In this case, people's actual work gives them a sense that they are contributing to something special. Not only does the employees' work matter to the company, but their part in the company's work matters to the world. This pride may come from the knowledge that their personal skills are being put to use in ways that benefit the greater good, or that the service they provide is of great value to other employees, clients, or the community. In some cases, this sense of meaning is palpable to employees. In the role of nurse, insurance adjuster, or pharmaceutical researcher, for instance, it is abundantly clear on a daily basis that one's work matters. In other cases, the leader must help to make the connection between an employee's work and the greater good.

As a leader, you can support employees' sense of meaningful or purposeful work by explicitly making the link between their jobs and some tangible or important outcome. One of the biggest missed opportunities for leaders is in failing to help employees "connect the dots" between their day-to-day responsibilities and the success of the workgroup or the organization. It can be as simple as asking employees "How did you change the world this week?" rather than "What cities did you visit while on the road?" As the saying goes, "People will work for money, but they live for meaning." And we have yet to find a company in which leaders can't find a way to accomplish connecting the dots for employees if they want to. A couple of examples illustrate this point:

- Agilent is a measurement company with expertise in electronic and bio-analytical measurement applications. The vision of the company is "To save lives and help people communicate." So whether it's testing 70 percent of all cell phones in the world (so that the handsets are perfect), or testing the air in the coal mines of China (so that they detect deadly gases, and hence save lives), knowledge of the life-or-death difference employees make is behind the efforts of each and every employee. Their internal website has pages full of stories about how their products help save lives and help people communicate. Employees are encouraged to read those stories and learn how their efforts contribute to our world.
- At Principal Financial Group, leaders at every level strive to help employees understand their role in the company's success. Leaders are provided with "Hot Topics for Leaders" kits with presentation templates, talking points, quizzes, and other resources to help employees better understand how their jobs support the company's mission.

The company holds contests encouraging employees to work with their leaders and write down how they contribute to each of the company's high-level initiatives. In one campaign, employees made and submitted videos showing how their roles affect the lives of customers, shareholders, and others.

- Medtronic manufactures medical devices, then delivers them to hospitals, so employees don't often have the benefit of interacting with the end-users or customers. So the company holds all-employee meetings and invites patients who received a device to come and share their stories. Often emotionally moving, these meetings allow employees to meet people who benefit from their work, and to see the impact of their efforts on patients' lives and well-being.

Perhaps your organization does not make medical devices, or isn't a health care organization. Perhaps your organization's mission is not to save the planet or change the world. Perhaps the people you lead have really difficult, demanding jobs that do not seem all that glamorous. Your response to these examples may be, "Well, that's all well and fine, but not where I work." But it is important to realize that every organization makes products or offers services that are needed somewhere by someone or by some other group. The important thing is to understand *why* the products or services are necessary and what they enable other people or organizations to do as a result of them. Often, considering the secondary or tertiary implications of what your products or services do is a way to identify the meaningfulness in the work.

We once went to visit The J.M. Smucker Company—marketers and manufacturers of fruit spreads, retail packaged coffee, and peanut butter, among other products—in Orrville, Ohio. We talked with employees during the facility tour. One of the line operators, when asked what her role was, exclaimed, "I help bring families together"—a nod to the company's stated purpose of "Bringing Families Together to

Share Memorable Meals and Moments." She saw the third- and fourth-order implications of her work and its potential impact on the lives of families that consume Smucker products. As a leader, consider the ways in which you can connect the dots. Smucker brings families together through their products. What higher purpose does your organization serve in the world?

PRIDE IN THE TEAM

An associate at W. L. Gore & Associates shared with us that "The things we accomplish in business are very personal for a lot of us. It's not just that I've accomplished a business goal with a team, and then I can just go home and shut my brain off and go about life as usual. A lot of the folks we work with become our friends and our family in a lot of ways, and when something good happens, we're going to celebrate the fact that we accomplished something. Sometimes, it's not just the destination; it's the journey." The team sub-dimension of pride examines the pride that employees develop in their team, the team's accomplishments, and their willingness to give extra for the benefit of the team.

Pride in the Team's Accomplishments
When people at a great workplace reflect on the work of the team, they experience pride in the collective effort of their workgroup or the organization and feel good to have contributed to the effort. Looking more closely at such companies, we see this sense doesn't just magically appear, but that efforts are made to support effective teamwork. Further, teams are encouraged to consider their successes and failures, and celebrate them. And finally, employees are often rewarded for their team's accomplishments.

Many companies utilize teams to accomplish goals, and they strive to create effective ones. At a basic level, this might include the use of team coaches or other organization development initiatives. But one thing that distinguishes the best workplaces are their efforts to create *spaces* where inspired teamwork happens. Better still if these spaces also reinforce the company's culture and goals. For example, eBay's company culture is reinforced even in routine meetings through their "Amazing Spaces" program. Buildings are themed by category, each representing something sold on eBay. The San Jose campus has buildings dedicated to Collectibles, Jewelry, Motors, Sports, and Toys. Within each building, each conference room is named according to items sold in that category. Employees within the Jewelry building might find themselves meeting in the Ruby, Diamond, Necklace, or Moonstone conference rooms. To take it to the next level, each room is given a budget, and employees shop for items on eBay that represent that particular theme. To that end, the "Ruby Room" is decorated with ruby slippers; a "Twister Room" features Twister game pieces on the walls; and a "Sweet Caroline Room" serves as a shrine to singer Neil Diamond. It takes a great deal of time and effort to create such an elaborate decorating scheme, not to mention the administrative costs involved with purchasing theme-related decorations. But it's well worth it. These spaces serve as a constant reminder of the very core of the business and help encourage an upbeat, creative work environment.

Mattel, the world's largest designer, manufacturer, and marketer of toys and family products, headquartered in El Segundo, California, also has spaces that reflect the ultimate goal of the team's work together. In their Design Center, instead of conference rooms, they have "play" rooms and an adult "playground" that includes a wide open space with rubber mats and large windows to create a meeting space that promotes connectivity, innovation, and the open sharing of ideas. Designers can also be seen traveling to and from the design space and throughout the department on bicycles or skateboards to allow for play during the workday. It is not uncommon for Mattel's employees in the Design Center to set up a Hot Wheels® racetrack or gather a group of employees for a competition with Mattel's hottest new game, as a fun way to inspire creativity with the brands.

Team efforts are not only supported, but also *celebrated* at the best companies. Coming together to reflect on the team's efforts encourages team pride. We often find in our work that with many companies, too many teams move from one project to another without taking time to consider the overall impact of the teams' efforts and celebrate their collective successes (or failures, for that matter—more on that later). Barely has the ink dried on the team's final report, and the team is being disbanded and repurposed, or it is taking on a new project. As a leader, you can encourage teams to take a pause, and consider the value of their efforts—and to do so in original, personal, and creative ways.

Take, for example, how QUALCOMM, a telecommunications company headquartered in San Diego, celebrates team accomplishments. Throughout the year, QUALCOMM hosts "employee trade shows," giving teams an opportunity to showcase and demonstrate their accomplishments to both fellow employees and senior management. Teams are able to convey their enthusiasm for their work, and to socialize and network with other employees outside their normal workspaces. These trade shows give employees from other parts of the company a chance to browse through new and upcoming products and technologies that are normally only demonstrated to external media and industry groups. As a result, teams develop a real sense of pride.

Another example of fostering team pride is seen in Microsoft's myStory competition, wherein individuals and teams were given an opportunity to submit a short video telling their own Microsoft story. Employees spoke about what they thought was unique about working at Microsoft, why it was a fun place to work, and how Microsoft enabled people to reach their full potential. In November 2009, they ran a myStory film festival that showcased the videos and awarded prizes to the winners.

A point worth repeating is that best companies tend to take an integrated approach to their processes and systems, and ensure that they align with the company's values. When companies indicate that they "value teamwork" but then only recognize or reward individual behavior, employees are left with an inconsistent message. Best companies put a premium on rewarding behaviors that are consistent with the organization's mission and values, including those of teamwork.

Giving Extra to Get the Job Done

Employees in great workplaces often share with us that there is an ethos of giving extra to get the job done. Likely, this ethos is an outcome of personal pride, but it also may inspire pride to see others share this extra effort for the good of the team. Team members are proud to see each other step up in order to make it happen, whatever *it* is. And they are proud of this quality. A short story by an employee at SC Johnson serves to illustrate what we mean by "giving extra":

> One of my responsibilities [on the Global Pandemic team] is a SharePoint site that is open to all global users. I had to change over the entire SharePoint site in very quick order to reflect a recent virus outbreak. I'm at work at a quarter to four o'clock one morning because that was good quiet time before all the phones went crazy and all the e-mails went crazy.
>
> I'm working on my site and my e-mail dings. There's an e-mail from a man by the name of Dan Horton, who is our Chief Administrative Officer. Dan had a question for me, and I answered him. About 15 minutes later, I get a phone call and it's Dan. "Oh my gosh," he said, "You must have the hottest seat in the world." He was just so great. I thought that was amazing. That didn't end. Later in the day, I get an e-mail from a leader, who says, "I just heard from Dan. I think you might need help. We're going to ask Kurt to free up some time. He's going to be all

yours." That's just the way we operate. Later, Dan walks into the conference room and he proceeds to thank me and the rest of the team for what we had done.

I tell that story because that's what it's like to work here. People know you. I didn't have to ask. They came. I didn't have to say a word. Here's Dan with his plate overflowing, and I'm just going to work until I get this done. If I work 20 hours overtime, so be it. It is an issue of helping people, and that's what my department does. The help was just like the cavalry coming. It was a great experience, I have to tell you, and one that we all have had, in some way or another.

Giving extra means that leaders recognize that extra effort is given by others to increase the value and output of the team. This is a special quality in great workplaces and is a sign of people's willingness to cooperate with each other and go beyond the immediate requirements of their jobs to create greater value. In today's business parlance, you could call this "discretionary effort." It's broader than just going the extra mile because of your own personal initiative or standards. Anyone can be a maverick. But in the best companies, a collective expectation for work that the team can be proud of is present.

We find that in great workplaces, employees understand that there is a give-and-take when it comes to support, and an "all for one, one for all" attitude. In this type of workplace, employees can feel confident going beyond their job descriptions. The extra effort is for the common good, and everyone has a role to play on the team. As a leader, it is important that you model this kind of behavior. Are you willing to "pitch in" and support your people shoulder to shoulder? It doesn't mean that you take on a new role, but it does mean that when the conditions call for it, you too give extra alongside your people in order to get the job done.

This kind of pride can be infectious. As a Wegmans employee relates, "Our part-time folks think of it as being a part-time career for them. They take it seriously and want to take care of business too; they want to take on the challenge. They will stay late, or give up their break, or work extra hard, or maybe someone who is not quite as involved will jump in and help, so they have each other's backs."

PRIDE IN THE COMPANY

Employees in great workplaces talk about pride in their jobs, and in their teams, but they also talk about pride in a third distinctive way: employees highlight their pride in the company's reputation and standing in the community.

When asked what makes their company such a great place to work, often the first things employees talk about are all of the cool or interesting things the company does, and that they are proud to be a part of such an enterprise. Often they share that they are proud of the company's products, mission, service, or people, as the following employee comments highlight:

- "For me, it's the quality of the product that we put out. At the end of the day, I think the result speaks for itself. I'm very proud of that."
- "I'm proud to work here because the core values and the envisioned future and the direction of the company as a whole matches what I feel personally. I think everybody in this group can say the same thing. We're all cut from the same cloth, and it makes me proud to know that the company I work for holds the same values that I do personally."
- "My pride grows with how we treat our employees and how we treat the rest of the world. That we set audacious goals about the impact we are going to make as well as audacious goals about our carbon footprint, about being good stewards of the earth."
- "I think what makes me proud about being a Gore associate is the two 'P's,' that's the people and the products."

- "We build great products, and when you talk to people and tell them you work at Google, they always have a story about how much they love the products and how much difference it has made in their lives. Also, the company takes some bold stands when it comes to innovation and certain principles it upholds, including 'Don't Be Evil.' There's a certain pride in saying that I am one of the people who works in that company."

The experience of company pride may be the result of its brand presence, its quality products and services, the role it plays in the community, or the cumulative total of factors we've already covered—leader's credibility, support and caring for employees, and a fair playing field. The important point is that in a great workplace, employees have a tremendous sense of pride in the organization and its impact in the world. Genentech is a biotech company that researches and manufactures therapies for serious illnesses. Drive onto a Genentech campus and it's hard to mistake what is important to them. Building exteriors, walkways, and stairwells are graced with photos of patients Genentech's employees have helped and a little something about their lives. It is a constant reminder to people that their work in their organization makes a difference, and it instills a great deal of pride.

Make no mistake: the organization itself benefits from pride. In great workplaces, employees talk about how they are proud to tell others that they work there *and* that they look forward to coming to work. We emphasize the "and" because we often hear employees at *good* companies say that they are proud of the company and will often tell others that they work there; but in *great* workplaces, they also follow that up by saying that they are excited to go to work in the morning. One employee shared with us, "I pass by a billboard ad for our company every morning on the way to work. I think, 'Gosh, we make cool stuff.' But then I get to the parking lot, and my enthusiasm just disappears." Unfortunately, his experience is not that atypical. And, as you might imagine, the gap between being proud of the company and looking forward to showing up costs companies money and goodwill, not to mention the hit to employees' emotional and psychological health. In great workplaces, companies are able to close that gap.

Employees at great companies also say that they want to work for their employers for a long time. It is not uncommon for employees at great workplaces to say that they even want to make careers there, and stay for the duration of their work lives. Employees in these workplaces tell us things like, "It's great to have a job where you say, 'I want to retire here.' Most people, they might job hop, but not here. My goal is to stay at Hoar Construction as long as they'll keep me, until I retire. I'm not looking for anything else. I think most everybody here would agree with that." While there may be a natural amount of attrition because of the company's industry or other factors, what is surprising is how infrequently we hear employees at great workplaces wanting to job hop to another company, compared with employees at other companies with whom we consult.

Some of these organizations have such a strong culture of organizational pride, that even when employees do leave for other destinations, they still have strong, positive feelings of those companies, much like people do after graduating from a school. And often these best companies capitalize on that. Bain & Company, a global management consulting firm, is a good example. The company strongly believes that its people and culture are its greatest assets, and invests significantly in maintaining, nurturing, and supporting its "alumni" network (people who used to work at Bain but have now left) by maintaining a global alumni database of all former employees so that alums can keep in touch individually. Bain also holds regular social and professional events for its alums. This benefits former employees by helping them to keep their networks intact, but it also benefits Bain. What better source of good hires than former employees? And in some cases, former employees are now Bain's clients.

Another aspect of company pride is the ways in which the organization gives back to the community. When the spirit of generosity pervades the workplace, it's natural for a great workplace to put a premium on giving back. One of the things we look forward to when visiting such companies is hearing about all of the ways the organizations contribute to their communities. Just as important, these companies also invest time and resources in getting *employees* actively engaged in volunteerism, community development, or other corporate citizenship programs.

Some best companies like Camden Properties, which owns and manages multi-family properties, or Publix Super Markets, which operate 900 supermarkets in five states, are literally a part of their communities, and invest heavily in those communities, in addition to engaging in other corporate social responsibility (CSR) activities. Other best companies take a broad view of being good corporate citizens, and encourage employees to get involved in whatever causes they are passionate about. The common thread in all of these companies is that there is a spirit of paying it forward. More than searching for a possible award for their CSR efforts, they view involvement as a right thing to do for their communities and their people.

In best companies whose industries offer less of a direct connection to their communities, we see a strong commitment to volunteerism, community involvement, and corporate social responsibility—sometimes from the moment they were founded. For example, outdoor gear and apparel cooperative REI has been on every one of the FORTUNE 100 Best Companies to Work For lists; their core purpose is to "inspire, educate, and outfit for a lifetime of outdoor adventure and stewardship." From the beginning, they took environmental stewardship seriously, and today they donate millions of dollars toward conservation and recreation efforts to local and national nonprofit organizations. Employees take great pride in knowing that their mission as a company goes hand-in-hand with their environmental and CSR (or stewardship, as it's referred to at REI) efforts.

Another best company, salesforce.com, a cloud computing company providing sales, customer service, and collaboration solutions, also integrated philanthropy from the very start. This is remarkable considering that the first few years of a start-up are often not ones that reap large financial benefits. Based in San Francisco, salesforce.com is a leader in on-demand customer relationship management (CRM) services. "The value of a corporation should be fully distributed not only to its leadership, but also to the communities in which it operates and the global community as a whole," says Chairman and CEO Marc Benioff. Marc developed and implemented the 1/1/1 business model—giving 1 percent time, 1 percent equity, and 1 percent product back to the communities the company serves. An additional 1 was added to represent being "one with the earth" and to implement a program to become a carbon-neutral company.

Whether or not community commitment is a founding value, companies can incorporate this element in a way that is true to their philosophies. As a senior leader at Hoar Construction offered, "We don't direct people to get involved in the community. That would be contrary to our values. What we do is that we give people help in what they want to do, and we hire people who want to do it. They're surrounded by others who want to do it. The momentum is there. We just try to provide opportunities." And in this way, Hoar is able to encourage their employees to get involved and connect them with opportunities to do so. Some ways that best companies get involved and encourage their people to find their passion include the following:

- Juniper Networks, a information technology company in California, considers their events as opportunities for team building and giving back to their community. Their Summer Picnic combines fun, team building, and charitable contributions, and also emphasizes using products that are good for the environment. Employees play carnival games to win prize tickets, which they can then drop into a box to give a Juniper Networks donation to the charity of their choice.

- Arnold & Porter LLP is an international law firm based in Washington, D.C. In addition to pro bono opportunities, the firm has a "rotation" or "loaned associate" program with public interest organizations that allows associates to spend six months working full-time for these organizations. For example, the firm has had a rotation with the Legal Aid Society of Washington, D.C., and the City Attorney's Office in Los Angeles, California.

- Based in Boston, Massachusetts, Bingham McCutchen LLP is a global law firm with 1,100 lawyers in 13 offices spanning the United States, the United Kingdom, Europe, and Asia. Their attorneys perform more than 61,000 hours of pro bono work, or an average of 77 hours per attorney. Bingham McCutchen has a dedicated group of staffers who cultivate and maintain pro bono opportunities; they have developed an intranet page with pro bono news as well as a Pro Bono Fellowship program that allows two associates to work full-time on pro bono work for a one-year period. The selected fellows support ongoing pro bono efforts and assist the public interest organizations the firm partners with in an attempt to meet the overwhelming demand for legal services.

- Whole Foods Market started the independent Whole Planet Foundation, which provides micro-loans to interested business owners in developing countries. In an effort to allow their Team Members greater interaction with the foundation, Whole Foods started the Whole Foods Market Team Member Volunteer Program, a 30-day in-country experience where the Team Members travel to the communities where they are sourcing products and providing micro-loans. The Team Members are able to learn some of the countries' languages and cultures, and experience the impact of micro-credit by meeting Whole Planet Foundation borrowers.

Whether your company was founded with a corporate social responsibility imperative, whether it is now developing such a focus, or whether such community involvement and volunteerism efforts are more organic and mainly driven by employees, as a leader you can support employee pride in the company's contributions to the community. One of the key themes that run through the various practices cited above is the clear commitment that leaders in these organizations make in advancing their CSR efforts and encouraging employees to become involved in such efforts. When employees see that their organization has a concern for the wider community of which they are a part, and are encouraged to support efforts that they are passionate about, the result is increased pride in the organization. In this regard, everyone wins.

LEADER IMPERATIVES

Here are other ways in which you can foster employees' pride in their individual efforts, in their team's efforts, and in the larger company.

Build Pride at Every Turn

At Analytical Graphics, the president compiles a weekly log of individual, team, and organizational accomplishments he hears about, witnesses, or comes across during the week, and he shares those every Friday at the weekly company lunch (yes, all 275+ employees come together every Friday for lunch and a short meeting). Whether it is an item he pulled from the local newspaper about an employee's efforts in the community, or a milestone that a team passed in developing a product, or how teammates pulled together to help one another out on a particular issue, he makes this a consistent practice. And employees feed off this energy. "Friday afternoon," one employee commented to us, "is always a high. What a great way to start the weekend, and make me excited to come back on Monday morning."

Support a Boundary-Less Organization

As a leader, help employees focus on the *collective* good. In great workplaces, employees will go above and beyond—working outside the normal scope of their roles and beyond the typical boundaries we see between departments or work teams. When this happens, people see their own team's connection with other teams, and they are proud of what those other teams can accomplish because they did their jobs well. When an employee at Google was asked about how his sense of pride in the company supported his efforts to get things done, he offered: "There is a culture of cooperativeness and a willingness to help each other out. There are not little fiefdoms. I've been at other companies. There are not little fiefdoms of, 'No, you do that so it's in your profit sector.' Or, 'No, you do that so that your headcount gets used up.' That's just not the way we do things here. The truth of the matter is, when you're in an environment that does do things that way, you are not aware of how much energy and productivity you're soaking up to protect those little fiefdoms, protect your ego, protect your status, and all those kinds of things." So help foster pride by supporting a more boundary-less organization.

Learn from Failures, Too

Leaders tend to focus on team and organizational "wins" as ways to increase levels of pride. In addition to doing this, it is also useful to celebrate "failures" in such a way that employees can learn from them and move on. Pride in the organization is likely to increase as a result of this. At Intuit, a software company located in Mountain View, California, the failure of a new business unit prompted the founder to throw a "failure celebration" party that publicly applauded the lessons learned from the 18-month effort. He showed how this learning experience would contribute to Intuit's future success, and subsequently assigned the leader of the failed venture to head the launch of another new business. At Intuit, and at other companies, celebrating failures is a way for employees to learn from mistakes, and move on.

Set the Tone
One of the most important things you can do as a leader is set the tone. As was suggested earlier in this chapter, *your* extra effort to get the job done and *your* contributions to community or volunteerism efforts speak volumes to employees about what is important. Sharing your own sense of pride in the company's products and services, and in the collective efforts of your people, also helps set the tone for fostering pride in individual, team, and organizational efforts and successes.

PRIDE BEHAVIORAL CHECKLIST

A behavioral checklist to encourage pride in individual, team, and company successes includes

Job
- I encourage people to share their unique skills and talents with the team.
- I frequently tell people how their unique skills and talents benefit the team and the organization.
- I help people connect their day-to-day responsibilities with the larger purpose of the organization.
- I help people understand how the work they do makes a difference.

Team

- I am a role model to my team for giving extra effort to help get the job done.
- I celebrate team accomplishments.
- I help my team to understand how our work together makes a difference.

Organization

- I encourage people to be a part of community events sponsored by the organization.
- I ensure that my team gets information about how our organization impacts the community outside of our operations.
- I ensure that people can see how their careers can develop within the organization.
- I help employees see their long-term future with the organization.
- I role model a sense of pride in the organization and its products.

WEGMANS FOOD MARKETS: PROUD OF THEIR CONTRIBUTIONS TO COMMUNITIES

Fast Facts:
- Retail Grocery
- Based in Rochester, NY
- Founded in 1916 by the Wegman family
- Privately held
- 39,000 employees in 91 locations
- List-maker since 1998, and also recognized in the 1993 book

Wegmans leaders take pride in doing the right thing. Food markets are, by design, a critical part of communities, but Wegmans employees take that part one step further by actively making a difference in their neighborhoods and cities. This activism is but one of the many things that imbue Wegmans employees with pride. The Wegman family still leads the company, and they have a firm belief that doing the right thing is more important than the bottom line. Colleen Wegman talks about the family values she brings to the organization in her current role as President. She says her dad (Danny Wegman, the previous President) gave her a piece of advice early on: "Lead with your heart, always do the right thing, always do what your customers would want you to do, and always do what you believe in. And then if it doesn't work out, that's OK, as long as you do the right thing and lead with your heart—make a decision that you can believe in and stand behind." Colleen adds, "That's always advice that I think has resonated throughout our organization."

Several times over, Wegmans leaders have taken actions that have cost them money, but undoubtedly they have reaped benefits in the way of customer loyalty and employee commitment. The most striking example is their decision to remove tobacco products from their stores in 2008. Though the move cost them $1 million in annual profits, cigarettes did not fit into their espoused "eat well, live well" philosophy. Danny Wegman, CEO, says, "We believe that there is not bad food. You can eat too much of any food, but it's not a bad food. We don't believe that a cake is a bad food; you just don't want to eat that much cake. But we don't believe that there is any good cigarette. What we like to do generally is start with our own people, and there are thousands of us now. We say, 'What is good for us?' And if it is good for us, it will be good for our customers too. So we reached a point where we were wondering how we could encourage our own employees to be healthy while we were selling cigarettes. So that was when we decided to stop." The community response was overwhelming, and largely positive.

Wegmans leaders chart the course for all employees to serve their communities, be it through incredible service or organized programs. A few examples of Wegmans' support of their communities include the following:

- Each store has a discretionary budget to fund requests from local organizations. Wegmans leaders believe that employees in the stores know their communities best, so store managers and community connection teams are designated to review requests and allocate funds.
- Initially launched internally as an employee wellness program, "eat well, live well" has now been expanded to other businesses in Rochester, Buffalo, Syracuse, and Hunt Valley, Maryland. Thousands of employees at nearly 400 organizations throughout these cities participate along with Wegmans employees in competitions to eat five servings of fruits and vegetables a day and walk 10,000 steps per day.
- In a typical year, Wegmans donates 16 million pounds of reclaimed food to local food banks and other agencies that feed the hungry. The company also has also raised over $14 million

since 1993 for hunger relief through annual Check Out Hunger and Care About Hunger scanning campaigns.
- In Wegmans produce departments, employees are educated and encouraged to share knowledge with customers about the importance of "striving for five" cups of fruits and vegetables per day.

Wegmans leaders also don't underestimate the importance of customer service when it comes to serving the community. As Jack DePeters, Senior Vice President of Operations, puts it, "We have one simple rule: incredible service. A brand new employee today can feel good about giving incredible service. They are empowered to let no customer leave our store unhappy. It's a simple message. I am not trying to send a rocket off to the moon; it's none of that stuff. It's just give incredible service." This is a message employees are proud to deliver on. When talking with employees, it is clear that they see themselves as part of something bigger than a grocery store. One employee, who has been with Wegmans for 24 years, says, "We really try to embrace the community and bring them in for events that are really an experience for them rather than just shopping for groceries." Employees at Wegmans are proud to be part of their communities, and they know that their leaders will do the right thing when it comes to keeping their communities healthy.

Case Study

W. L. Gore & Associates: An Innovative Culture and a Culture for Innovation

Fast Facts:

- Product Development and Manufacturing for Fluoropolymers, Including Electronic, Industrial, Medical, and Fabric Applications
- Based in Newark, DE
- Founded in 1958 by Bill and Vieve Gore
- Privately held
- 9,000 associates in 30 countries
- List-maker since 1998, including recognition in the 1984 and 1993 books; recognized internationally fifty times

W. L. Gore & Associates is an innovative organization, and they've built a culture to support that characterization. While not everyone is a fit with their unique way of operating, those who are take pride in their workplace. At Gore, people are just as proud of the culture as they are of the products they produce, and it shows.

One of the most striking elements of Gore's culture is that nothing seems to be an either-or. They create an "and" when making decisions; they don't need to settle for choosing one way over the other. This leads to some unconventional choices, like getting rid of anything that stands in the way of innovation and creativity, including job titles, job descriptions, and rigid organizational structures. Employees are called associates, a leader is defined as anyone who has followers, and sponsors (not managers) guide your career. While leaders understand the importance of their culture, they know it doesn't exist for its own sake—Gore is a wildly successful company. As CEO Terri Kelly puts it, "Having a strong culture doesn't mean having a soft culture. . . . You're really doing it to serve the business purpose. We've really tried to make that linkage because if you're not careful, you'll have a population that gets anchored around the values culture and having a nice work environment, but aren't willing to do the kinds of things that keep the enterprise healthy."

Gore leaders know that if you are going to choose a spot outside of traditional business practices, you also need to choose your words deliberately so people know what is expected. And you need to foster an environment where everyone is both guided by and a steward of the core values and the strategic goals. As Terri Kelly notes, "You're really put to the test of matching what you'd like to do from the business perspective and how do you make sure it matches with the culture so there's consistency. And our associates will tell you very instantly when you're getting it wrong." Without clear communication and widespread stewardship, Gore's unique practices would be fascinating, but not necessarily effective. Gore has found a way to make its culture not only effective, but also fundamental to success.

Here are some of the unique practices in which associates take pride:

- Hiring takes culture fit into account. To be successful at Gore, you must have a desire to pursue opportunity without a fixation on title or status. In other words, candidates must be driven, but not to climb a predetermined ladder. They must make their own way in a boundary-less structure. Gore also looks for people who are team-oriented, and uses teams of associates to evaluate candidates.
- No more than 200 people are located in any one of their buildings at any given time. While buildings are located close to one another in order to share services, Gore leaders believe that business benefits arise from the camaraderie and informal communication that comes from keeping things small. People can't hide in a small, cohesive organization, and they are more likely to keep up with current communications when these can be targeted to smaller groups of people focused on common goals.

Case Study

- Open, direct, two-way communication is ingrained in Gore's culture. Associates with questions or concerns are encouraged to go directly to the person with the answers, whether it's a teammate, team leader, or the company president. Associates answer their own phones and leave their doors open.

- Associates select the projects they wish to work on. As long as there is a business need for their skills and passions, Gore associates have the freedom and the responsibility to increase their contributions while building their expertise. While formal classes and performance discussions are held, associates are free to innovate in their career paths at Gore as much as they innovate in product development.

- At the outset of each project, associates and leaders ask four key questions: "If I succeed on this project, will it be a contribution to the enterprise?" "What is success with this project?" "How will I know when I have succeeded?" and "Who will want to celebrate 'success' with me?" If associates and leaders can't come up with answers to these questions, they know the project's value is limited.

These practices directly impact associates by creating an environment they are happy to work in and contribute to—and one that they champion. An associate with Gore comments, "I had only been here about eight months to a year, and one of my teammates was listening to another person on my team complain about something. She looked right at her and said, 'What are you willing to do to make it better?' I thought, 'What a powerful question!' It just stopped that vein of the conversation dead in its tracks and started a turn towards finding a solution. That kind of atmosphere is sort of contagious. It really is."

CHAPTER SIX

CAMARADERIE

"The people here are great!"

An example of how Scripps works as a family—When I first moved out here, I had been married less than a year and had inherited three teenagers. Four months later my husband got deployed. So, new area, new mom, freaked out husband in war zone. My coworkers totally rallied around me, totally rearranged my hours so that I never had to be the early person so that I could get the kids to school, never had to be the late person so that I could be there when they got home from school. They kept me sane.

—SCRIPPS HEALTH EMPLOYEE

In great workplaces, people believe their coworkers see them as complete individuals, with families and hobbies and passions outside of work. They have fun, and they celebrate both personal and company milestones. They see themselves as one large team, and they go out of their way to cooperate and help. It is these foundations that lead to a friendly work environment, one that is welcoming to new and transferring employees alike. We've arrived at the aspect of a great workplace we call Camaraderie.

While leaders certainly establish their own relationships with employees, they also indirectly influence the Camaraderie of the entire organization. Though less direct, these influences are no less important. Employees tend to enjoy one another more when they are competent and a match for the organization's unique culture, so the effectiveness with which a leader hires not only influences his or her Credibility, but also may plant the seeds of Camaraderie. Leaders may create and facilitate a new employee's onboarding, which provides a context for other employees to greet and orient new members of the workgroup. Leaders may plan celebrations, budget funds for them, or simply attend them as a way to support the closeness of the workgroup. And, lastly, a leader may role model a broader definition of "team" by assisting other workgroups or departments, or engaging in collaboration beyond his or her immediate workgroup.

Even if a leader hires well, plans celebrations, and creates an integrated welcoming process, people won't spontaneously build strong relationships with one another unless they trust their leaders. Leaders cannot force or control the Camaraderie relationship, but they can work to inspire trust. Without trust, people are less likely to be authentic; rather, they watch the leader for cues and signals as to what is appropriate. More energy directed at figuring out the leader's position and expectations means less energy focused upon developing close ties with coworkers.

Of course, we've also seen leaders protest at the other extreme; they wonder why camaraderie is important at all. They may argue that their workgroup is too busy, their industry is too buttoned-up, or their people are too far-flung. It is at this point that we remind leaders that, like all other aspects of a great workplace, camaraderie looks different wherever you go. Take Aflac, for example. While the actual customer issues employees handle are not often a cause for celebration, Aflac takes time out to celebrate its people. Employee Appreciation Week is a jam-packed week of activities that includes something for everyone. During a recent Employee Appreciation Week weekend, employees and their families at headquarters spent the day at the Georgia Aquarium, tested their mettle at Six Flags Over Georgia amusement park, or breathed in the country air at the Butts Mill Farm. Employees in New York had a choice of fun at Six Flags' Great Escape and Splashwater Kingdom or a brunch cruise on Lake George. Employees in Columbia, South Carolina, attended a family movie day, while employees in Omaha, Nebraska, visited Worlds of Fun Amusement Park. Aflac covers all expenses for the family activities. During the workweek, leaders host a free breakfast and hold daily prize drawings. The week culminates with blowout bashes, where employees can win trips and cash prizes, play games, and simply have fun.

Contrast this with how Sun Microsystems in Argentina builds fun into their daily work. Sun Microsystems is a leading worldwide provider of technology, solutions, and services for corporate computing. Every time a specific group meets a target or goal, the successful employees ring a golden bell in the main corridor. After hearing the bell ring, all employees go immediately to congratulate and celebrate the success together. The celebration often continues after work, as employees offer their congratulations and toast to their achievement.

When employees feel a sense of camaraderie with their coworkers, they feel as energized by their work environment as they do by their non-work environment. They bring all of their skills to the table, and they readily help each other accomplish organizational goals. When relationships at work are strong, it also allows employees to focus more readily on their goals. Any ancillary worries about family issues impacting the work environment or difficult decisions and conversations are lessened because people are in a supportive environment, and this allows even greater productivity. When productivity ends with a celebration, it builds even stronger ties, and the cycle begins again. In sum, the degree of camaraderie an employee experiences, along with trust and pride, only serves to deepen the employee's relationship with the organization. An employee from Wegmans says, "There's a network that you form with people, be it in your department or in the programs you are working. There are people who you spend a lot of time with, so they become your sounding board, your second family if you will. You hear people make references like, 'This is my Wegmans family,' people who are there for you and care for you and carry you through so many different things in your life."

In this chapter, we break Camaraderie into three separate parts: intimacy, hospitality, and community.

INTIMACY

It's a sign of intimacy when employees feel they can be themselves at work, and when people at work care about one another. Note that this is different than a sense that *management* cares (which was covered in Chapter 3, "Respect"). Intimacy is the sense that people care about their coworkers, and it is signaled in a variety of ways. People may celebrate special events together, both personal events (such as birthdays and new babies) and company-wide milestones. Employees themselves describe Intimacy best:

- "Something very significant, I recently transferred from ICU to Short Stay and two weeks after working there, I found out that I had to get surgery. I was out for a month. While I was in the hospital I received this card: 'Mai Mai, thinking of you and wishing you a speedy recovery. You are missed by your new Short Stay family. From, Barbara Maria and staff.' And even a bouquet of flowers. I keep this card on my kitchen counter where I can look at it all the time."
- "We have a strong culture of people who respect each other, who treat each other well, providing good customer service and doing the right thing. That helps to build a relationship. Culture is like a relationship. You have a family here. We all learn to live and work together well because we spend a lot of time here."

- "I just get a little choked up about this because it is just like a huge family, you know? It really truly is a great place to work. I love this company. I have never been treated this way before. Personal experience: my wife lost her father one day and people from work had sent us really nice food in a basket and told me to take as much time as I needed. Four days later, her mother passes. So I am worried about the job and I have got to get back and this, that, and the other, and the response of my coworkers was to 'Take as much time as you need.' A month later my brother passes and I thought, 'All this love coming from Camden; they really care.'"

Leaders can take action to foster strong relationships among their workgroups. First and foremost, they can attend celebrations, even if they don't plan them. This happens at SC Johnson, where an employee reports: "I call it touchability. I think the uniqueness of our senior management across the board is not only approachability, but touchability. Someone had a baby shower in the Developing Platform, and Steven Stanbrook, the COO, was an active participant in a baby shower. It just resonated with me, 'Wow! That doesn't happen anywhere.'" When leaders are involved, they show their support for events that build camaraderie among team members, and in doing so they build caring relationships of their own.

Programs that allow employees to show caring for one another often reach employees at their most vulnerable times: when their safety is at risk, when they've lost loved ones, or when they are in transition. A few examples of unique programs seen at the best companies:

- JM Family, a diversified automotive company headquartered in Deerfield Beach, Florida, shows its concern for associate safety in the event of a hurricane or other crisis by implementing "Department Calling Trees." The phone trees are an organized way to determine the safety status of all associates in the affected area. Additionally, they mobilize their Associate Volunteer Search and Restoration Teams. These teams actually go to the homes of associates who had not been successfully contacted via the Calling Trees, and who had advised that they needed assistance with tasks like putting up blue tarps for their leaky roofs or removing tree limbs that blocked the entrances to their homes. All volunteers receive appropriate training, including in the safe use of power tools.

• One of the main ways in which The Men's Wearhouse supports its employees in times of need is through the Willie Lopez Emergency Assistance Fund. The fund was created in honor of Willie Lopez, a beloved district manager who died suddenly, leaving his wife and three young children in desperate financial straits. It provides financial assistance to employees across all divisions who have fallen on hardship as the result of tragedy, and is funded solely by employees across all divisions who voluntarily have money deducted from their paychecks each week. Since its inception in 1998, over $3 million in grant money has been disbursed.

• SAS sends a standard obituary notice to all U.S. employees when an employee dies, and provides a website for employees to leave notes of condolence. This website allows SAS employees to grieve and remember their colleague in a very special way. After a couple of weeks, SAS prints the responses and makes them available to the family members of the deceased, to let the family know that the deceased was an important part of the SAS family.

One of the more unique practices for fostering intimacy comes from Plante & Moran, an accounting firm based in Michigan. They have a departure tradition that extends at least 40 years: the "green" departure memo. Any staff member, regardless of position, who is leaving the firm for a new career or personal opportunity, writes a departure memo. Memos are then reviewed, printed on green paper, and posted on bulletin boards (or their electronic bulletin board) throughout the firm. Departure memos are typically Oscar-type acknowledgments ("Thank you to everyone I ever met at Plante & Moran . . .") combined with details of the departing staff member's immediate and long-term plans. Particularly interesting are memos of staff members who leave the firm for decidedly non-CPA-type positions—priest, doctor, disc jockey, Oscar Meyer Wiener mobile driver, actor. There's no question these memos are cathartic for employees, but they are surprisingly eloquent, humorous, and touching as well. Leaving an employer can be awkward and bittersweet, but Plante & Moran's departure memos allow people to leave their work families with gratitude and grace.

Lastly, to help people feel as though they can be themselves, leaders might create programs and contests to showcase the non-work talents of their staff. Or they can simply provide a forum for employees to express themselves. We've worked with companies that asked their green-thumbed employees to design landscapes, their artistic employees to submit artwork, and their musical employees to provide entertainment for company events. No matter the industry, we see leaders encouraging employees to let their talents shine.

- KPMG hosts an amateur photography contest. Partners and employees share the photos they've taken during their vacations for the chance to win some great prizes. The grand prize winner is determined by KPMG partners and employees across the firm, who vote for their favorite photo using an online voting process. The grand prize winner receives a $3,000 vacation voucher.
- Mayo Clinic Rochester boasts of its own singing sensation: the Stairwells. The group comprises employees from Mayo's Section of Patient Education who enjoy singing and found that the only place they could gather to practice when they first started was,

you guessed it, the stairwell. They originally organized to fete colleagues within their work area when a special event was observed, such as someone's retirement. Word got around, and Mayo Administration and other departments began to invite them to sing at institutional and departmental events. A popular request is their "Mayo, One Mayo" song, which is sung to the music of "The Banana Boat Song" or "Day-O." The Stairwells incorporated the Mayo mission and values into the lyrics in a fun, entertaining way.

HOSPITALITY

The second aspect of Camaraderie is Hospitality, referring to both the friendliness and fun in the work environment (Enjoyment), and the degree to which new employees are welcomed (Welcoming). Both serve to create a warm working atmosphere, and employees feel stronger ties to the organization in this type of environment. While work is a place to meet individual drives for achievement, creativity, and livelihood, work can also serve as a means to meet the social needs of belongingness and friendship. From an employee's first day on the job, the best workplaces are inviting and pleasant.

Enjoyment
While people often think of a fun working environment as one of formal celebrations and events, true enjoyment often comes from the little things. An employee at Hoar Construction puts it this way, "I don't think it has to be a special event. It's just coming to work. The offices are stacked in there together, and you better like that guy next door and be willing to have fun with him because you're going to be listening to most of his conversations. Just going to lunch—everybody gets together to go to lunch and have a good time and talk about things. We count down the

days to football season. It's just the atmosphere." The Container Store has a good example of celebrating in a small, yet meaningful way. In order to show support and appreciation for moms and dads who work on either Mother's Day or Father's Day, the company purchases corsages and boutonnières for these parents to wear during their shifts. While enjoyment doesn't have to be programmed or scheduled, at a minimum it has to be supported and encouraged by trusted top leadership. In fact, much of the enjoyment experience can't be programmed or scheduled.

Nonetheless, some companies, like Perkins Coie and Deloitte, go above and beyond to ensure enjoyment. Both are in largely professional industries, where lightheartedness is not the prototypical characteristic of the work environment. One of law firm Perkins Coie's unusual and unique traditions is their Happiness Committees. Happiness Committees are small, self-appointed, and self-governing committees within offices and departments whose members are not known by others. They perform anonymous, random acts of kindness, such as leaving gifts at workstations. Deloitte, on the other hand, is a New York–based professional services firm. They have an online social and professional talent networking tool—DStreet—which allows all the firm's people to create online profiles, search for others, and ultimately strengthen their networks and sense of community. DStreet allows people to upload and share other professional data as well as photos, favorite music, a current reading list, recipes, and the like. It even has a blog so people can wax poetically about their passions. Both are examples of more deliberate actions taken on the part of leaders to facilitate fun and friendly work environments.

Welcoming

The first few days a new employee spends with an organization is a crucial time. It is during this time that employees begin to build relationships, garner commitment to the company, and understand the importance of relationships at work. Upon accepting a new job, people are energized and excited. Great workplaces channel that excitement through new employee orientation programs, new hire mentoring, and check-ins with new employees at various intervals after they start. Some even begin the welcoming process before employees' first day. Through a sort of alchemy, new job excitement is converted into commitment to the organization. You will know that you and your workgroup have welcomed employees in a meaningful way when they cannot wait for the next new hire so they can be a part of the welcoming committee!

Best companies build upon the basic necessity of orientation in many ways. Some begin the welcoming process before employees even sign a letter of offer. Boston Consulting Group has such a practice. Each prospective hire is assigned a "captain"—a BCGer who is responsible for developing a deep one-on-one relationship with the prospect and helping him or her through the decision-making process. The captain answers all questions and acts as a navigator through BCG, putting the prospective hire in touch with all relevant parties to ensure questions are fully addressed and to help him or her meet a diverse group of BCGers. Captains are typically at the principal level or above, emphasizing the importance put on making sure prospective hires have access to the resources they need to assess fit.

Once an employee is hired, great workplaces ensure he or she begins to build relationships with others in the organization. Many managers encourage their employees to take new hires to lunch or to spend one-on-one time with the new hires. Others assign buddies or mentors to ensure that each person has a single go-to person for questions and concerns. Other companies take an organization-wide approach that includes a formal welcome published in newsletters or on the intranet. One of our favorite practices comes from CXtec, a New York–based reseller of networking and voice equipment. In their "donut cart" program, on the first Friday of every month, new employees who joined within the previous month walk around the office to deliver donuts and coffee. This tradition provides a great way for new employees to meet other seasoned employees and experience CXtec's culture.

Building relationships with senior leaders is also important. NetApp holds a TOAST (Training on All Special Things) program for new hires every month, led by NetApp's CEO, Tom Georgens. TOAST features presentations from at least six of their top executives, including the CFO, the senior VP of Human Resources, the CMO, the vice chairman, a founder, and others representing every major business function. At lunch, participating executives are joined by a number of vice presidents, who each sit at a lunch table with TOAST attendees, essentially giving new employees a one-on-one opportunity to have lunch with a senior level executive within their first month on the job. As one NetApp employee puts it, "Having the CEO, president, founders, and other top-level staff conduct the new hire orientation makes an amazing impact. It helps new hires to feel appreciated, drives ambition, and sets the tone for the work environment."

At some companies, the fanfare wears off quickly, but the best companies ensure the entire onboarding process does not end so abruptly. Many have some type of check-in process, whereby the new employee gives and receives feedback on the experience so far. At OhioHealth, a key component of the welcoming process is "Right at 90," which ensures the newest team members adjust comfortably to their roles. During their first 90 days of employment, new associates meet regularly with their manager on an informal basis and receive feedback about their progress and performance. At the end of 30, 60, and 90 days of employment, new associates receive evaluations of their progress from their manager. At the end of an associate's first 90 days, the associate and his or her manager are invited to a Right at 90 celebration, which is an opportunity to mingle with senior leadership, share experiences, tell stories, and celebrate the new associate's desire to succeed. New associates are encouraged to bring family members and other close friends to celebrate their successful completion of a milestone event in their continued journey of growth. Not only do such programs as the one at OhioHealth ensure the employee's success within the organization, they also further build commitment and provide suggestions for building greater Camaraderie through the orientation process.

Before we leave the topic of welcoming, consider the special case of welcoming acquired employees. While in many cases, acquired employees are happy to join a new organization that is more financially sound or well known, that isn't always the case. Moreover, large numbers of employees are brought in at once. And those employees already have established relationships with their original organization, so the welcoming company has a more complex task than welcoming a group of employees who purposefully and willingly applied and chose to join the organization. Often, the first step to success in these situations is to understand the unique needs of acquired employees, and to create opportunities to build relationships with employees in the new organization. Some examples of successful practices follow.

- When CH2M HILL, a Colorado-based engineering consulting firm, acquired the Alaskan-based oil and gas firm VECO, the company made an extensive effort to make the new employees feel like a part of their new company. Within weeks of the acquisition, virtually every former VECO employee attended face-to-face orientation presentations in locales as far away as Prudhoe Bay, Alaska; Sakhalin Island, Russia; Fort McMurray, Alberta; and Dubai, United Arab Emirates. In addition, as part of the acquisition, employees received grants of CH2M HILL stock, making them not just employees, but owners of their new company.
- Valero Energy Corporation, which owns and operates refineries and gas stations, has a history of acquiring other refineries. In order to smoothly assimilate the employees from newly acquired refineries,

senior management personally welcomes new employees, provides information on Valero's workplace culture and benefit programs, and answers questions. Specifically, when a new facility is acquired, the CEO hosts a welcome barbecue. In addition, Human Resources holds informational sessions and benefit enrollment meetings for employees in all shifts and for their spouses.

• QUALCOMM recognizes that employees from newly acquired companies have specific questions and concerns. Thus, they make a great effort to appropriately address those questions and make the employees feel welcome and integrated into QUALCOMM. Extranet websites are created for each acquired company to introduce them to QUALCOMM history, culture, and resources, as well as to provide detailed answers to questions about their benefits and other employment-related issues. In addition, the employees receive custom welcome packets and a customized on-site orientation session. Follow-up integration surveys help measure the success of their integration and identify areas that require attention.

Welcoming employees in thorough and deliberate ways helps build relationships, deepen commitment, and further the social rewards of being a part of a group. It also positions employees for success by giving them more tools and resources to navigate their first few months on the job. Finally, it helps to build a larger sense of community, which maximizes cooperation and collaboration.

COMMUNITY

In the best workplaces, employees cooperate with one another, but not only because their job requirements or the organizational charts mandate that they do so. Rather, they feel a broader sense of team, and that everyone is working together to create a great product or provide a great service. As illustrated in employee quotes earlier in this chapter, sometimes employees feel as though they have a second family at work, one where both the joys and the challenges are shared. Leaders, for their part, can role model and tie cooperation to the values of the organization.

Aflac uses its famed duck to remind employees of the importance of the "flock" and to create a sense of cohesion among its people. You can't hear Aflac without thinking about the famed "Aflaaaac!" duck, and you can't travel too far on campus and within buildings without seeing him. He's a source of great pride and inspiration within Aflac. A duck pond sits at the visitor's entrance of the Paul S. Amos Campus. Toy Aflac ducks line every office and cubicle. On jean Fridays, Aflac T-shirts prominently displaying the duck are the norm. And every time a new Aflac commercial airs, employees get a sneak preview of the latest duck escapades on the company intranet and on TVs in lobbies. A sense of family is built into the culture at Aflac, both through their internal values and their external marketing campaigns.

We also see leaders at the best companies creating opportunities for people in different departments to work together. This creates an appreciation for what employees do across the organization, but it also helps employees to understand how the quality of work in their department affects those in other departments. A few examples:

- Support staff members in Whole Foods Market office facilities are occasionally able to work alongside store Team Members. Usually, these support Team Members are invited to "help out on the floor" of a nearby store during busy holiday seasons or when a store department team wants to go on a team-build and is unable to cover the necessary shifts using other local stores' Team Members. Office Team Members don aprons, hats, and buttons and help out by bagging groceries, collecting baskets and carts, stocking shelves, and assisting customers. This fun opportunity helps give office Team Members—especially those who have never worked in stores—a perspective on what goes on in the stores, and creates a connection between office and store staff.

- At Scripps Health in San Diego, both administrators and managers have schedules that allow them to visit with individual units and departments, and to talk directly with staff who hold various schedules. The "rounding" schedules help administrators and managers to be accessible 24 hours a day, 7 days a week, including early morning and late evening shifts, which builds trust. By communicating on location with employees responsible for patient care, leaders get a better understanding of what employees do and how departments interact. They can make suggestions and broker conversations between departments. Not only does rounding support cooperation between administration and patient care, it provides information that helps to better interdepartmental cooperation.

- At EOG Resources, an oil and natural gas company, employees are dispersed across numerous locations. To help employees with similar positions connect and collaborate, the company holds annual conferences for different technical divisions, including Drilling, Exploration, Completions, Production, Reservoir Engineering, EH&S, Landmen, and Accounting. By holding these conferences, the company not only shares information from all locations and at various levels within the organization, they also help employees establish meaningful relationships with their peers from other locations. Building these connections makes it easier for employees to collaborate in the future. It's always easier to pick up the phone and ask a question when you know the person you're calling.

The more employees understand the work of different departments, divisions, and locations, the more they are able to view them as part of an organization-wide team, instead of groups competing for resources and recognition. At CH2M HILL, cooperation is not only part of their culture, but also an expectation of all employees. CH2M HILL supports employee cooperation through a structure that connects people of similar disciplines, but leaders also make it clear that employees are responsible for their own network. As one employee puts it, "The people in my discipline group reinforced the fact that you should be able to find the right answer in three phone calls. If you can't get the right answer in three phone calls, that's an indication that something's not right. That's still true today. If you know how to cooperate, this organization works well for you. If you haven't figured out how to do that or you resist doing it, it may not be the right place."

Today's work environment is one of greater dispersion among workers, and it's busier than ever before. Given this climate, many companies take advantage of social networking tools and knowledge management systems in order to create a greater sense of family and team. Sometimes, social networking technology is used to connect people for business purposes or in the recruiting process. Other times, connections are for more personal reasons. In either case, employees are better connected to one another, and this affords greater opportunities to cooperate. Consider examples from Accenture, General Mills, and salesforce.com.

- Accenture is one of the world's leading management consulting, technology services, and outsourcing organizations. By providing every employee with a personal webpage, called Accenture People, employees at all levels are able to communicate contact information, biographical details, and other information about their professional expertise to the entire company. Accessible from the internal homepage of Accenture's Portal, it also allows employees to share relevant personal information, such as universities attended, and photos, hobbies, and skills. Accenture People is a great opportunity for all employees to learn about and connect with colleagues and leaders across the company.

- In an effort to appeal to younger applicants and interns, General Mills piloted a page on Facebook for interns to connect and build community. According to their chief staffing officer, the site positioned General Mills as a "cool employer," and they discovered that the site was heavily utilized by the interns prior to their arrival and for the first few weeks while they settled into their roles.

- For most of the technology industry, online social networking has become an important factor in meeting and getting to know each other, both professionally and personally. For salesforce.com's Recruiting Team, it's no different. Their future employees are tech-savvy, and the best way to reach potential new hires is often through one of the many social networks available, such as LinkedIn, MySpace, and Facebook. These types of social networks offer recruiters a way to move beyond the gatekeepers in college career development offices to find and build long-term relationships with potential new hires.

Building community through role modeling, formal programs, and social networking allows employees to feel more a part of their organization, and furthers cooperation among people. When successes are celebrated, even more Camaraderie is built. In this way, a positive, productive cycle begins anew.

LEADER IMPERATIVES

Your most powerful tools when it comes to building camaraderie are not as explicit as those in the other chapters of this book. While you may build strong, personal relationships with employees, that serves to increase trust in *you*. On the other hand, Camaraderie refers to ties *between employees*, and the only influence you have is in hiring people with a natural affinity for one another, creating and supporting opportunities for employees to connect, and role modeling the behaviors you'd like to see.

Hire Connectors

By hiring people for culture fit, you are already halfway there when it comes to Camaraderie. If people are selected on the basis of the values they share with the organization, they are more likely to connect with others. Employees in great companies are acutely aware when new employees just don't fit. Diversity is important, and should also be pursued in hiring, but not when it comes to shared values and culture. For example, The Container Store touts a commitment to a well-rounded company. One of their philosophies is a focus on teams. They communicate to managers that "We work hard in our recruiting efforts to hire only great employees who can work together to do incredible things. The warm, open culture of our company supports a team-oriented environment. We celebrate successes together, as a team, and work toward the same goals." Their Chairman and CEO, Kip Tindell, says, "When it's done right, being part of a team is one of the most beautiful of all human experiences."

Create a Context

Though you cannot fully manipulate the degree to which employees welcome or care for one another, you can put vehicles in place for them to build their camaraderie. As an example, consider the Mentor Program at Camden Property Trust. The program provides one-on-one training to new employees during the first 90 days of employment by utilizing coworkers in the same position to provide hands-on training to new employees and assist in familiarizing new employees with

Camden's culture. CEO Keith Oden refers to mentors as "ambassadors of the culture."

You can also support the use of employee-supported funds and other channels for expressing concern. Since 1999, the CUP (Caring Unites Partners) Fund at Starbucks has assisted partners with financial support in response to unexpected events such as the death of a loved one, fire, or natural disaster. Starbucks partners support the CUP Fund with personal contributions, and all Starbucks partners are eligible to apply for assistance. In total, the CUP Fund provides millions of dollars to thousands of partners each year.

Role Model

A quick way that we can size up the degree of Camaraderie in any organization is to listen for a higher proportion of "we's" than "they's." When people feel a part of a family or team, they will use the word "we" to describe successes and challenges. The larger their sense of family or team, the larger the sense of "we." Sometimes people see the entire company—thousands and thousands of people—as part of the same family. Other times, we notice a much more frequent use of the word "they," even when referring to people in their own company, or their own work-group. Sometimes leaders preface sentences about employees by saying, "These people . . ." Whenever there is a prevalence of "us versus them" language, we suggest that leaders need to build Camaraderie.

The more you can use "we" to describe people in your organization, the more people understand themselves to be part of a larger team. "They don't understand us in Phoenix" becomes "We need to arrive at a better understanding with the Phoenix office." "These people don't understand" becomes "I wonder what is standing in the way of our communicating with one another." The subtleties of language can shift your perspective, while also sending signals to employees about the reach of cooperation that is expected.

Build Trust

Building trust is probably the most important imperative. Sometimes leaders choose to put a great deal of effort into building Camaraderie at the expense of building trust with people. Helping to foster strong relationships between employees is an important aspect of building a great workplace, but trust is foundational. Once you've built trust, employees will better accept the leverage you do offer with regard to Camaraderie. When employees trust their leaders, they give new hires the benefit of the doubt. They participate in events and activities to build relationships. And when leaders espouse the merits of a workplace that is one big family instead of competing factions, employees believe them.

CAMARADERIE BEHAVIORAL CHECKLIST

A behavioral checklist for building Camaraderie includes

Intimacy
- I express my beliefs and concerns openly while doing what is best for the organization and the team.
- I attend celebrations that my team organizes.
- I encourage people to be themselves, and to respect the individuality of others.
- I encourage people to celebrate special events.
- I provide resources and time for my team to celebrate their accomplishments.
- I take action to help people in times of need.

Hospitality
- I take care to hire people who have a good balance of cultural fit and unique contribution.

- I coordinate or support activities to help new and transferring employees feel welcome.
- I encourage my team to take time out of their day to enjoy their coworkers.
- I ensure that new hires are warmly welcomed to the team.
- I go out of my way to make new hires feel welcome.
- I help to create and maintain a relaxed atmosphere in my workgroup.
- I take opportunities to bring fun to our work.
- When someone transfers to my department, I warmly welcome him or her to the team.

Community

- I create opportunities for my team members to meet other people in the organization.
- I encourage and reward cooperation in my workgroup.
- I ensure that everyone on my team understands how the work of other team members creates value.
- I foster a warm and supportive group spirit in my team.
- I help people to keep focused on the greater good in addition to our own individual or group interests.
- I show respect to people in other departments throughout the organization.
- I consider my team members to be more than just casual acquaintances.

CAMDEN PROPERTY TRUST: BUILDING A FUN COMMUNITY FOR EMPLOYEES AND RESIDENTS

Fast Facts:
- Real Estate Development and Management
- Based in Houston, TX
- Founded in 1982 by Ric Campo and Keith Oden
- Publically traded under the symbol CPT
- 1,750 employees in 203 locations
- List-maker since 2008

Camden Property Trust owns and manages multi-family properties in 13 states and the District of Columbia. While factually accurate, this description does not tell the full story of what Camden does. They specialize in communities—efficient and responsive communities that are also fun and friendly. And what works for the Camden brand also works for their culture. Two of Camden's nine values are "Team Players" and "Have Fun," and you can see these values being played out all over Camden—both in major events and over the course of the typical workday. What's more, Camden employees genuinely care for one another.

Events that create the Camden employee experience are numerous, but the most highly anticipated is Camden Skit Night, which takes place every year on the first night of their annual Management Conference. Leaders from regions across the U.S. come together for information sharing, team building, awards, and of course the skits. Skits are created by teams of people across the company. As the company has grown, the skits have become more elaborate and now involve months of planning and advanced audio and video components. The skit tradition allows employees to interact on a different level, without titles or job roles. Employees develop skills and talents they never knew they had—acting, directing, writing, critiquing, video editing, song selecting, costume designing, mediating—the list is endless. This tradition allows people to develop and excel in areas that may never apply directly to their day jobs but provide personal fulfillment and a strong sense of accomplishment. The tradition has been around just about as long as the company itself, and it's an event where senior leaders and managers alike take the stage by following the example set by Camden's leaders and founders, Ric Campo and Keith Oden.

According to Oden, the real value in the skits lies in the teamwork it takes to pull one off. He said that the process of creating a skit is fundamental to a team's ability to work collaboratively and make decisions—regardless of title or tenure. And employees' naturally competitive spirit keeps the bar high, so all groups treat the challenge as one of great importance. The fact that the skits keep 450 people entertained each year is "just a by-product." What really matters is that by creating the skits, employees create lasting relationships that enable them to function more effectively and seamlessly as a team. And with over 20 years of skits recorded in the company's archives, leaders have captured the evolution of a corporate culture now recognized as one of the greatest in the United States.

Additional evidence of the fun and friendly environment at Camden is not hard to find. Whether in the course of their daily work or as part of a mentorship program, Camden's people create a culture that is the very picture of camaraderie.

- Camden takes time to celebrate accomplishments and holidays. Halloween is a no-holds-barred departmental competition at the corporate office. Department workspaces have been transformed into a haunted house, Old McDonald's farm, a bird sanctuary, Aladdin's palace, a hunting lease (Camden reports that no animals were harmed), Benihana, and sets from *Sister Act* and *The Addams Family*. The winning department gets a pizza lunch and, more important, year-long bragging rights.

- Camden's employees love to play jokes on one another, and the pranks they pull are not only an example of fun in the workplace, but a testament to the strong relationships between employees. As an example, Elizabeth, a project engineer, kept hearing a doorbell sound while she was working. She asked everyone around her if they heard it, but nobody did. She checked everyone's cell phones for a doorbell ring tone, but found none. On the second day, she stopped by to see her coworker Nathan, a project manager. She told him she had to go home for lunch to escape the doorbell sound in her office. Nathan responded, "You mean the sound you hear when I press this button?" Because Elizabeth had teased Nathan about the irritating ring tone on his Blackberry, Nathan went to Home Depot, purchased a doorbell kit, hid the chime in the ceiling above Elizabeth's desk, and placed the doorbell on his desk, which he pressed periodically throughout the day. Her coworkers who denied hearing the doorbell? You guessed it. They were in on the joke!

- Even onboarding at Camden is accomplished through relationships, as seen with the Mentor Program. During the first 90 days of employment, a worker gets hands-on training from a coworker in the same position. The mentor also assists in familiarizing the new employee with Camden's culture. Keith Oden refers to mentors as "ambassadors of Camden's culture." The Mentor Program provides development opportunities not just for the new employee, but also for the tenured employee who is selected as a mentor. Camden mentors undergo an application process and complete a tailored training program conducted at corporate headquarters.

Employees who feel part of the Camden family are more likely to create a community for Camden's residents. One employee, who was also a resident for nine years prior to joining the company, explained it to us: "I have never worked for a company where the founders have come to me and hugged me and said thank you for doing a good job. So by them doing right by us as employees, we pass that on to residents. We don't have apartment complexes. We don't have units. We have communities. We have apartment homes. And I tell people that if you want to live in just an apartment complex, you are going to have to go down the street, because we are family."

Fostering good relationships internally also leads to efficient operations. Again, a Camden employee says it best: "If there is not an answer you need right on-site, or if you are the only one there that day, you can pick up the phone or send an e-mail to our business support center and they are always happy to help. Or you can call another community manager on another property, and you feel very supported in all aspects. You never feel like you are bothering anyone, everybody is willing to share their stories or give their ideas." Creating an environment of fun and camaraderie makes Camden a great place to work. The fact that it spills over into the resident experience at Camden is what makes them successful in the marketplace.

Note: Much of the material for this case study is from an unpublished manuscript by Jessica Cross Rohman, a consultant at the Great Place to Work Institute.

MICROSOFT: GENIUSES WELCOME

Fast Facts:

- Information Technology—Software Development
- Based in Redmond, WA
- Founded in 1975
- Publically traded under the symbol MSFT
- Approximately 90,000 employees in 108 locations around the globe
- List-maker since 1998 and recognized in the 1993 book; recognized internationally 198 times

There's only one place in the world where a company welcomes you to campus with a concierge and a place to collect your thoughts before your interview, channels your enthusiasm once you are hired, and then encourages you to move freely about the company. It's Microsoft, and they have good reasons for their warm welcome. Lisa Brummel, Corporate Vice President of Human Resources at Microsoft, says, "Attracting and retaining talent is the number one job we have. We're an IP company built on the people. At the end of the day, if you don't have the right people, it's very hard to succeed. For me, it's critical that this place be the right place for a very wide variety of people to come and work, whether it is age, nationality, area of expertise, business interest, or customer focus. This place has to appeal to the best and the brightest because that's how the business is going to move forward."

If the best and brightest come with high standards about what they expect to see in the recruiting stage, Microsoft delivers. Just to name a few of the ways people are introduced to their potential employer:

- The "Experience Microsoft" space at the Redmond headquarters is a place for recruits to start their day on campus. It showcases Microsoft's latest technology, provides "touch down centers" for people to print their résumés or check e-mail, and provides video clips of Microsoft employees talking about their experiences. If the space isn't cool enough on its own, it also houses the Microsoft concierge who, in her own words, "makes people feel at home." The concierge and others in her position help candidates learn their way around Seattle and find good restaurants and attractions, and offer anything else that they may find important to learn before accepting an offer that might be made.

- There are Xbox games set up in the lobby to encourage interaction among candidates, and Microsoft Surface tables loaded with special applications just for recruits.
- For the recruits who can almost "see themselves" at Microsoft, the Experience Microsoft space also offers technology that allows them to see themselves at Microsoft—literally. On one of the computer displays in the space, recruits can choose words and phrases that describe them, have digital photos taken, and later see themselves and the words to describe their experience artfully displayed on the wall.

Scott Pitasky, Corporate Vice President for Microsoft's Human Resources Talent & Organization Capability group, talks about three things that are important in recruiting at Microsoft: candidate experience, sharing information, and the Microsoft brand. "First, we are fanatic about candidate experience—from providing a concierge who can suggest cool restaurants and things to do for candidates visiting Seattle for the first time to talking about the technology that we have—we want the experience to be great. Next, we want to arm our candidates with great information to make an informed decision, and one of the ways we can do that is by sharing information on our global candidate website. We've listened to what candidates want to know while they're interviewing for Microsoft—from what it's really like working here, to sharing stories about how employees are able to grow their careers and follow passions outside of work. It's our way of putting ourselves in a candidate's shoes and helping them get to where they want to go. The last thing is that we are very cognizant of ensuring that we are investing in our employment brand. Try to find a person in the world who doesn't know Microsoft or Bill Gates. We think it's important to add to what people know about Microsoft by being transparent about what it's really like to work here, what makes us special and how we see the exciting customer and business challenges ahead of us."

Young employees talk about their experiences discovering the real Microsoft as well. According to one of them, one of the most pleasant surprises is how go-getting and receptive to their ideas leaders are. "One of my mentors in Zune said, 'You know what? We are the leading edge of technology, but us senior people, GMs, SVPs, we're dinosaurs. You're a year or two out of college. It's your responsibility to make sure you push your managers, make sure you push the company, and make sure your voice is heard.' I think [new people may think], 'Oh my god, these people have been here for 15 years. They're running enormous business units. They can't possibly value what I have to say.' But that's not true here."

Just as important, Microsoft doesn't reserve the wow-factor for their welcomes for new employees. Employees are encouraged to move within the company, and this is a major perk for a dynamic, entrepreneurial workforce. Again, an employee says it best, "People do talk about what they're going to do next. I have this thing, and my management knows it, that I kind of ramp up for a year and a half, and then I reassess with all these different products. I ask myself what skill sets I want to go to, is my job helping me achieve those skill sets, and that type of thing. There's a lot of openness around the opportunities, and I see it as part of my job to keep my eyes open to those so I stay excited about my work." Microsoft is big, but not "corporate." And the ways in which they welcome new recruits and employees to campuses around the world are but one part of how this shows.

CHAPTER SEVEN

GLOBAL PERSPECTIVES

Great Workplaces Around the World

Not too long ago, our German office considered making a change to one of the statements on our employee survey. The survey asks whether employees view their workplace as a "fun" place to work, but the German researchers in that office believed that an exact German translation of "fun" might not make sense from a German cultural-work perspective. They considered a series of other options, and determined that they would substitute "deep joy" for "fun." Weeks later, when the surveys were returned and reviewed, researchers noted an interesting pattern. While the word "fun" had indeed been changed in the survey itself, in the section where employees are invited to add commentary in their own words, those at the best companies used the word "fun" to describe their work environment. What we see from this story is that though culture, language, and locations may differ, the Model provides a surprisingly (even to us sometimes!) stable framework for understanding the employee experience across great workplaces.

Indeed, one of the most important insights we have learned over the years in studying the best companies is that great workplaces exist regardless of size, industry, or location. We hear similar themes whether we ask employees at a large corporation in Germany or a small family business in Chile the following question: "Is this a great place to work, and if so, why?" This is largely because the Model is based on needs and values—trust of the people you work for, pride in what you do, and enjoyment of the people you work with. The needs and values represented in the Model have universal appeal, and so there is much in the employee experience, regardless of country, that is common and consistent.

That said, there are also considerations unique to multinational corporations and companies based in other countries. The Institute currently has a presence in over 40 countries, and is well represented in the Americas and Western Europe. We also have a growing presence in Asia and Oceania, Africa, the Middle East, and Eastern Europe. Our experience working with large and small organizations around the world has taught us some valuable lessons in applying the Model. Mainly, while the Model provides a portable framework for understanding the workplace, there are several questions that often arise regarding the international application of it. In this chapter, we explore some of the most common questions and issues—our international FAQs—and show examples of how the Model's principles apply all over the world.

ARE THE BUSINESS BENEFITS OF THE MODEL THE SAME ACROSS THE WORLD?

In the first chapter, we noted that best companies are more productive and profitable than their peers. We offered several examples of the business benefits that accrue to organizations that develop high-trust work environments. And we shared the results of how the best companies in the U.S. stack up compared to the S&P 500 index. But what about companies not located in the U.S.? How do they stack up? To begin with, similar studies of how the best companies to work for in Brazil, the United Kingdom, and Denmark compare against their local stock market indexes all reveal that great workplaces outperform their peers. But that's just the tip of the iceberg.

The Great Place to Work Institute Europe regularly analyzes a number of key business metrics of the companies that make the 100 Best Workplaces in Europe list. And, as you might expect, the best outperform their peers. Palle Ellemann Knudsen, European Managing Director, notes that when they compared the 100 Best with the 100 companies that participated in the 2009 study but returned the least positive survey results (the 100 Lower), the best companies outperformed in a number of areas:

- The 100 Best grew at twice the pace of the 100 Lower.
- Absenteeism was 70 percent higher at the 100 Lower.
- The 100 Best received twice as many job applications.
- The 100 Best developed more new products.
- The 100 Best had lower voluntary turnover.
- The 100 Best increased revenue by 23 percent but staff by only 11 percent.

Further evidence of the Model's universal business benefit is found in research conducted in Institute offices around the world—research based on comparing lists of best companies with individual consulting clients. The cumulative picture that emerges is the same as what we see in the U.S.: investment in creating a great workplace yields significant dividends for the organization. For example, the Great Place to Work Institute Chile measured the progress of a long-term retail consulting client, and evaluated the positive impact of trust, pride, and camaraderie across several financial indicators. Researchers looked at issues including employee theft, product damage, and staff turnover. At the outset, they determined that the deficiency in trust across the organization was costing this organization about $19 million annually. Working to improve its trust level, the company was able to realize $58 million in cost savings over time.

As another example, in Germany, the Great Place to Work Institute conducted a research study that compared workplace culture and economic success of organizations from different industries and sizes. A representative group consisting of 37,000 employees in 314 companies was compared with the group of best companies in Germany. The research demonstrated several things. First, there is a large difference between the best companies and the representative sample in terms of workplace trust, the former rating much higher. And second, the research demonstrated that up to 30 percent of the difference in economic success between the two groups was attributable to workplace culture (and guess which group was more successful?).

In these examples, we find that not only is the Model portable across the world, but so too are the potential business benefits that accompany a focus on workplace culture.

HOW DO YOU CREATE A CONSISTENT CULTURE ACROSS A MULTINATIONAL COMPANY?

As consultants, we often are asked this question by leaders at large, multinational, diverse firms. While there are no easy answers to this question, we know from experience that the best multinational companies invest considerable time and energy in ensuring that the "core" experience of the organization is similar across the globe, while providing flexibility to local country leadership in addressing unique needs.

Ensure a Core Experience

Let's first look at the first part of that equation—what we mean by "ensuring a core experience." In great workplaces, leaders are fairly clear about how they intend to win in the marketplace, and they understand what kind of culture is required to deliver on that strategy. They have answered the question "What do we want our employee experience to be like?" and they have crafted policies and *global programs* that support their frameworks.

Microsoft Corporation provides an excellent example of an organization that has committed itself to being a great workplace wherever it operates. In 2009, Microsoft made the list in 24 countries where the Great Place to Work Institute recognizes the best workplaces. While there are many reasons why Microsoft has been so successful, it's worth looking at one specific program that ties the employee experience in its hundreds of locations together: "The New World of Work." Microsoft's mission is to enable people and businesses throughout the world to realize their full potential, and one aspect of that potential is to help companies re-imagine how work can be accomplished.

In 2005, Bill Gates launched The New World of Work Initiative, which was intended to help organizations around the world to improve their work processes and productivity. The program is especially alive and well at Microsoft itself, where Microsoft people are given laptops and smart phones, enabling them to work from anywhere, at any time. As a result, most Microsoft offices *all around the world* encourage flexible scheduling, and many employees work from home one or more days a week.

"The everlasting search for improvement in how we work and the wish to be authentic in everything is unique for a commercial company like this one," wrote an employee from Microsoft Netherlands. "The New World of Work connects vision with technology and behavior and leads to a better balance between work life and private life."

An employee at Microsoft Belgium also shares enthusiasm for this program: "The New World of Work gives us complete flexibility to determine in a creative way how to do our projects and when we want to work," she wrote. "This gives me energy every day. It allows me to treat my family the way I want. It gives me the opportunity to do a number of things regarding my health and sporting activities. The way things are delegated allows me to work in a flexible way and to combine my job at Microsoft with my tasks as a mother."

Microsoft has created a culture where having a great workplace is fundamental to business success. And The New World of Work is a framework that ensures that core experience, whether the employee works in the Netherlands, Belgium, the U.S., or Hong Kong, or travels between them. And what is the basis of that culture? Trust, of course. Microsoft's Senior HR Director for Western Europe, Frank Abbenhuijs, says that regardless of nation, Microsoft's culture all comes down to a consistent focus on people and trust. He adds, "Trust is not connected to one culture, but rather it is a worldwide language that makes people work together."

Like Microsoft, best companies create a core experience in a variety of ways. Significantly, leaders in the best multinational companies make a habit of sharing best practices across their network, bolstering the creation and establishment of a core experiences. Many companies we have worked with share best practices through structured events like leadership conferences where people from around the world gather together. Participants benefit as much from sharing their experiences with others as they do from information provided in the presentations. Qliktech, a leader in business intelligence software, which was founded in Sweden and is now based in the U.S., convenes an all-employee conference. During its latest conference, all employees from across the globe (close to 600) came together for several days to learn, plan, and share. Other organizations, such as Novartis, a pharmaceutical company based in Switzerland, create their core experience through leadership development programs where emerging leaders are transferred to different countries or business units to gain experience.

Balance Corporate Strategy with Local Customs

While they are very determined on establishing universal values and essential corporate programs, the best multinational firms give their subsidiaries a lot of freedom in adjusting policies and practices to local culture and custom. In contrast to having top-down, headquarters-driven strategies, the best multinationals tend to encourage innovation of practices at the subsidiary level and actually stimulate a healthy competition among subsidiaries for creating the most effective practices that their colleagues want to replicate. For example, Cisco's Environmental Awareness Campaign raised awareness of environmental issues and Cisco's green strategy by encouraging employee participation on and during the week of Earth Day. Earth Day events were held in 21 locations globally, so the program encouraged camaraderie at the local level as well as around the world. Cisco employees were able to use their Cisco WebEx technology to link in with each other during the week. Cisco also encouraged employees to participate in Earth Hour, at 8:00 P.M. local time on Earth Day, wherein cities, households, communities, and businesses are invited to turn off their lights for one hour to show that it's possible to take action on global warming.

Teamwork, innovation, fun, and giving back are a part of Cisco's core values, and they help shape its culture. Events like Earth Day give Cisco employees an opportunity to collaborate, develop greater camaraderie, and give back to the community, and they form an important part of Cisco's workplace environment. So, while the focus is global, the implementation is local. This "glocal" approach is one way to ensure a core experience.

NEITHER MY COUNTRY NOR MY COMPANY IS VERY BIG. IS IT STILL POSSIBLE TO CREATE A GREAT WORKPLACE, AND IF SO, HOW?

What underlies this question is a sense that a company has limited resources from which to draw. This isn't necessarily an issue that affects just international companies; even in the United States, smaller companies do not have unlimited resources to put toward some of the programs and perks we have identified in this book. Yet it's a particularly relevant question in countries around the world with smaller GDPs, or where the human resource infrastructure is not as well developed.

First, it is important to understand that the point of this book is that it's *trust*—not money—that defines a great workplace. Small companies can create great workplace environments by changing their approach to how they leverage the time and talent of their people, which costs nothing at all. But we would also offer that what financial resources you do put toward the development of your people should be laser-focused. In this section, we give two examples of companies that have mastered this focus. Piscines Ideales, the first, is a small Greek company that designs, constructs, and maintains swimming pools. The second, Reaktor Innovations, is a privately owned software and technology consulting company based in Helsinki, Finland. They each have been recognized as one of the best companies to work for in Europe. However, both are relatively small companies operating in smaller economic environments, and both companies do not have large HR departments. While creating a great workplace within the constraints of a small company, each has done a stellar job of putting resources exactly where they belong—in service of creating a great workplace culture.

Piscines Ideales

Stelios Stavridis, the CEO of Piscines Ideales, was scheduled to return from a business trip on the night before his birthday. When he arrived at his house late at night, he found a group of his company's employees, with birthday hats, whistles, and a poster, waiting to sing him the birthday song—at midnight. What would compel such dedication to an organization's leader? For employees at Piscines Ideales, the answer is obvious: it's all about family. And that is the core of how they view their company's culture.

"I think our team spirit and enthusiasm proves that we are a happy family with strong bonds!" wrote one employee. "I really feel that I have a second family, and I am more than proud and happy to be a member of Piscines Ideales!" While many small companies benefit from a sense of closeness, the 135 employees of Piscines Ideales take the "extended family" spirit to a new extreme. The company's annual conference is called the "Family Gathering." And CEO Stavridis—whom employees refer to as "Captain"—serves as a doting father figure for all his company's people.

Of course, as any good family does, Piscines Ideales helps its members to grow and thrive. The resources that they do put forward are in service of employee growth. For example, through an annual "job rotation" program, employees are able to spend a few weeks each year in different departments to gain a more holistic understanding of the company, and the company also pays for master's degrees for employees who seek further education. This approach actually saves money as they do not have to develop a large, internal training and development program. Further, Piscines Ideales has a structured process for helping employees take wing as entrepreneurs by opening their own franchises. Through a formal program open to everyone, employees who want to launch their own Piscines franchise businesses can receive training, funding, public relations support, and other resources.

While Piscines Ideales does put resources into creating a "family" culture, the outcomes of their efforts are priceless. The culture itself begins to support behaviors that contribute to a great workplace . . . free of charge. "I really feel that we are a family," wrote another employee. "In difficult times there are people to help you and to be there for you. When you need encouragement, they encourage you. When you need comfort, there is always someone to comfort you. When you celebrate your success, again there is always someone celebrating with you. And when you feel lost, someone is there to give you directions."

Reaktor Innovations

Reaktor has never carried out any HR development activities. Instead, they live and breathe being a great workplace. Reaktor's 130 employees are primarily engineers and consultants who develop software for large public and private organizations. Reaktor holds as its mission a desire "to combine cutting-edge technology with an uncomplicated, human approach." This might explain the fact that fewer than ten employees have left the company since it started back in 2000. Again, we see how a laser focus can make all the difference.

Because its business relies on maintaining high levels of technological expertise, Reaktor places a strong focus on professional development. The firm's exceptional training is rooted in the CEO's philosophy that the company can—and must—continue to improve. "Our goal is to build the best expert company of the world," says Chief Executive Officer Vesa Lauronen. "Being number one in the 2008 European Best list means we are doing something right. However, we believe things can always be done better."

Reaktor empowers its employees to train each other: the company is organized to let the experts at Reaktor share their own fields of expertise like user interface training or testing. Reaktor also holds Open Space every six months in which employees in small groups discuss all practical issues regarding working as well as work environment and company development.

Reaktor also has internal coaching services, which means that teams can request that an expert from another team come in to work with them to build their skills. And the firm sponsors training camps on such topics as sales skills and coding languages; about two-thirds of employees participate in these camps, even though they are often held on Saturdays. Managers and employees uphold a strong working team through constant communication. Teams sit down once a month for a "retrospective," a feedback session to reflect on their progress and areas for improvement, and the company's intranet includes online discussions and blogs for people to voice their opinions and exchange professional information. Everyone in the company meets each month for a meeting, and employees can suggest topics for the agenda. The company also sponsors a variety of employee clubs to ensure that employees maintain strong relationships. None of these activities require significant financial resources, and none of these activities necessitate being a large company.

So, if you are holding this book, and you are part of a small company in a village in Peru or a town in Croatia, realize that it is your approach to your people—not the resources at your disposal—that will determine how your employees experience the work environment.

HOW CAN I ADDRESS CULTURAL DIVERSITY AND INCLUSION?

In Chapter 4, "Fairness," we discussed the issue of justice as an important aspect of our Model. We noted that best companies tend to be cutting-edge in their efforts to ensure just treatment of employees. Here we turn to the more complex issue of how these same principles apply in an international context. From our work with large multinational corporations (MNCs), and our experience with our own affiliate offices around the world, we are sensitive to the unique issues that arise from working in a globally interconnected world. But we don't perceive these issues as a "challenge" in the traditional sense. Instead of seeing diversity as a problem to be dealt with, we see it as an opportunity to help your organization grow.

While the Model applies regardless of nationality and cultural context, *how* it applies will look different, and leaders need to work toward an acceptance of each individual's cultural customs and standards. An employee from Google tells a story that shows the leeway in best companies for employees to be themselves no matter the cultures they hail from. He says, "This morning I was chairing a global meeting. We had people from everywhere, and on a wall you can see all their images because we were video conferencing. There was this person from the Paris office that was on the call, and one of his coworkers came in, and she probably didn't know that he was on a video conference. She kissed him goodbye. All of a sudden, people stopped because there was kissing activity going on one of the screens, and I didn't quite notice it. So we made fun of it, and I said that I missed it and asked if they could do it again. He called her back, and she came and did it again, and she waved at the camera. People had a good laugh and moved on. I'm just using that as an example to show that there is an irreverent aspect to it that is very refreshing and very welcome. At the end of the day, we are just humans coming to work, and we bring all of our essential humanity to work. That brings a lot of fun to the workplace." While the cultural standard of kissing each other goodbye doesn't apply everywhere, the ability to accept differences in cultural standards is a new frontier for diversity in multinational companies.

Historically, PwC's vision of equality was to treat everyone the same, whether they were white males working in India or Indian women working in the U.S. But over the last ten years, their philosophy has evolved. When leaders talked to their people, what they heard was that differences matter. And they matter all the time. To achieve true equity, the firm needed to acknowledge differences and create a more customized experience for everyone. This was a major mindset shift in what they thought it would take to create a great place to work, and it required them to have much more candid dialogs about diversity. Ultimately, their goal is to create a culture where individuals are valued for the unique contributions they bring and are able to achieve at the highest levels.

Michael Fenlon, a Human Capital Leader at PwC, offers, "We live in a world that is much more interconnected globally and culturally, and you are much more likely to work with people from different backgrounds. We expect our professionals to collaborate effectively with people from other countries with different life experience, and across differences in language. So, the world has changed, and that in turn has led us to focus on building the cultural dexterity of our people." As a result, PwC has worked diligently in creating an inclusive culture. One example of their effort is PwC's "Global Mobility tour." Global Mobility provides employees with the opportunity to work for a member firm of the PwC global network on an international assignment and rewards participants with opportunities to work with global clients, strengthen their cultural awareness, create global networking, build relationships, and improve knowledge and skills in a particular area of focus. "By creating opportunities for other PwC network firms to send their employees to the U.S. firm and the reverse, we enhance client service and create goodwill among the network firms and greater opportunities for all our people," Fenlon says. A long-term assignment is typically two to three years, while a short-term assignment is up to a year. As a result of efforts such as this, PwC's 160,000 partners and employees in 151 countries across the PwC network are able to learn from and support each other to meet client needs.

Telefonica O2 UK Ltd, one of the U.K.'s largest telecommunications providers, gives us an example of how an organization has worked to develop a culture of inclusion. The company's Diversity and Inclusion Programme was introduced to recognize the benefits of a diverse workforce. Based on employee feedback, a number of new initiatives led by the Diversity and Inclusion Manager were rolled out, including:

- Ensuring that the workplace at O2 is a diverse and inclusive environment where everyone feels respected and included. To help with this, a diversity and inclusion e-learning module was introduced for all UK employees to complete.
- Prayer rooms in all key locations, which have a high proportion of ethnic minority employees.
- Religious festivals and holy days highlighted on internal calendars along with accompanying information about the history and significance of the holidays.
- Halel meat options in regional canteens. In one location, during Ramadan, training times are arranged to accommodate new starters, and a trainer is provided to allow employees to break the fast.
- Work with Asian Development Association of Bury, a town near Manchester, U.K., to promote roles within the local Asian community.
- Work with Shaw Trust, a national charity, to provide work opportunities for people who are disadvantaged in labor markets due to disability or ill health.
- Introduction of a reasonable adjustments policy and toolkit to support current and prospective employees with disabilities, and to support their managers too.

Telefonica O2 UK Ltd's diversity and inclusion efforts move beyond the typical programs we see in many of our clients. The examples we note above are extensions of a diverse workforce—wherein the company responds to the real and valued needs of its employees. And working in an international context, creating a sense of inclusion becomes an important component in a successful business strategy, as we noted in the first part of this chapter.

I'VE LIKED HEARING WHAT COMPANIES HAVE DONE TO INCORPORATE THE MODEL, BUT I'M CONCERNED THE SAME THINGS WON'T WORK IN MY COUNTRY OR IN SOME OF THE COUNTRIES WHERE MY BUSINESS HAS OFFICES.

Most of the time, a good idea is a good idea. A program that employees love in Germany, they'll probably also love in Argentina. In this section, we want to give you some inspiring examples of programs that have worked well in different parts of the globe, and the areas of the Model they follow. As you can see, they have much in common with programs we've highlighted elsewhere in the book. Indeed, that's the whole point.

Credibility in the Netherlands

&samhoud is a Netherlands-based consulting firm that has built a strong employee culture focused around a mission to "achieve breakthroughs by inspiring and connecting people." The concept of "connection" runs through the entire organization. Last year, a group of Sammies (as the company's employees are known) travelled to 14 cities around the world—Utrecht, Beijing, Berlin, Brussels, Buenos Aires, Istanbul, Jerusalem, Cape Town, London, Madrid, Moscow, New York, Paris, and Tokyo—to explore the concept of connection by passing around 10,000 blue balls to strangers, engaging them in spontaneous play. This kind of travel-based learning occurs frequently at &samhoud. Within their first year on the job, new hires are sent out to trek with their peers along the medieval pilgrimage route to Santiago de Compestella, in Spain; the trip is designed to reinforce the power of interpersonal connection and one's personal journey. And in early 2009, a group of Sammies flew to the U.S. for a trip themed around "Entrepreneurship"; they capped off the trip by attending the inauguration of Barack Obama. To explore "Creativity," they attended an arts festival on the Dutch island of Terschelling, and groups of Sammies have also traveled to Greece for a trip based on the theme "Know Yourself."

Respect Throughout Europe

In Europe, McDonald's collaborators can create "training passports" for themselves. Each passport is a personal document, and belongs to the employee. The passport takes an inventory of an employee's diplomas, track records, and training. It also contains written comments by the employee so he or she can keep track of his or her experience. Another tool that employees can use is the "McPassport," which is available to all European employees. It allows each employee to apply to live abroad and to work in another European Union McDonald's restaurant. In this way, employees at McDonald's can see the tangible evidence of the company's efforts to provide training and development, and it provides an easy reference should a McDonald's employee wish to move and find a similar job in another city.

Fairness in Canada

Becton Dickinson Canada Inc. (BD) is a global medical technology company that designs, manufactures, and markets new products. BD Canada sells a range of medical supplies, lab equipment, and diagnostic products. Traditionally, BD offered employees three additional vacation days to celebrate the Christmas season. But at the recommendation of a participant in their diversity training program, management has since amended this policy to be more inclusive. They still offer the extra vacation days—but they are now called "diversity days" and can be used at any time of the year to recognize the celebration of all culturally based holidays.

Pride in the United States

Medtronic is a global leader in medical technology, alleviating pain and restoring health. One statistic they are very proud of is that "Every four seconds someone's life is saved or improved by a Medtronic product." Their work and mission are vital. The importance of the mission is emphasized in the Mission and Medallion ceremony that regularly takes place on-site in many locations around the world. In this ceremony, the chairman of Medtronic visits the site and meets with newly hired employees to discuss the importance of their mission. He then presents employees who have been with the company for over six months with medallions showing the Medtronic symbol of the rising person and the wording of the mission. In this way, the corporate goal of creating pride gets attention at the local level.

Camaraderie in France

Soccer is very much anchored in the company culture of Danone. The sport is used to share and to live Danone's values and also to allow as many Danoners as possible the opportunity to meet through the Danoners World Cup. Every two years, the company organizes the Danone World Cup, a soccer cup for all the employees worldwide. In 2010, almost 12,000 employees battled for the tickets of the final game that takes place in Athens (Greece) for the 8th edition. Participants are invited to a barbecue after the local championships, which promotes the team and family feeling between the local companies and subsidiaries.

These are but five examples of programs throughout the world, and they could probably all be shuffled. Camaraderie in the Netherlands might focus on speed skating instead of soccer, and Respect in Asia might focus on externships instead of passports. Again, the point is in the inherent flexibility of a good idea.

LEADERSHIP IMPERATIVES AND NEXT STEPS

In all workplaces, employees come to work seeking leaders who are believable, hoping that they are respected enough to be set up for success and expecting that they will be treated fairly and with dignity. They want to have pride and meaning in their work, and they want to have positive relationships with the people they work with. Regardless of where in the world you find yourself, employees seek very similar things. Whether used in Poland, or the UAE, or Argentina, the Model provides a useful framework for considering the elements that employees seek in a great workplace. The issue for you as a leader is that while employees in all of these places seek informative communication from their leaders, how this is done may vary in each country because of local culture and context. The task for you is to create the policies, programs, and practices that are relevant to your own country's cultural context.

Develop an Inclusive Mindset

Developing an inclusive mindset will go a long way in capitalizing on the talent in your organization. If your role is to interact with colleagues and customers from other countries, developing cross-cultural sensitivity is key to being successful in the global, interconnected economy we now find ourselves in.

Balance Global Consistency with Local Creativity

Be clear about what elements of your company's culture are core to how you do business and, therefore, need to be consistent across the organization, and which elements can be left up to local creativity and innovation.

Learn from Best Practices in Your Organization

Remember that best companies also put into practice systems for learning from the best workplace practices from their offices around the world because good ideas come from everywhere.

Instead of ending this chapter like the others, with a behavioral checklist, here we offer several questions for you to consider as you apply the Model in an international context:

- Am I clear about the core elements of my company's culture that need to be replicated across all of the countries in which we operate?
- How do we learn from our internal best practices globally?
- How can I use our country's culture, history, and celebrations in service of creating a great workplace?
- Do I have a plan in place for learning how to effectively interact with employees, colleagues, and customers in different countries?
- Do I have a plan for learning how to interact effectively with the diversity of our organization in my own country?
- How can I learn from the best companies in my country (or in the region) to create a great workplace here?

CHAPTER EIGHT

TAKING ACTION: CREATING *YOUR* GREAT WORKPLACE

earning about the Great Place to Work Model, and how each dimension lives and breathes within organizations that have been recognized for their trust, pride, and camaraderie, is the first step toward creating a great culture. Still, just as with snapshots from a summer vacation, the Model shows us some beautiful and exciting things, but not how to get there. Like a trip to any destination, your journey will depend upon your starting point, the vehicles at your disposal, your resources, and the number of people who are coming with you. And no matter how precisely you plan, you can never know what the next miles will look like until you've begun.

If you feel daunted, you aren't alone. We've seen managers become paralyzed by what seems like a large gap between them and the best. Eventually, they determine either the challenge is too large or the timing is not right. Sometimes, they want to create change, but demand more information and data to create next steps, and then become mired in the information they've collected. We've also seen managers attempt to address all of their gaps at once, taking actions that go too far, too fast. Sometimes, they end up damaging trust because they force an action that the people in their organization are not prepared to handle, like implementing flexible work hours when the company doesn't have the technology to support it. Neither paralysis nor mania is an approach we'd recommend.

Instead, we recommend leaders take measured and thoughtful action that moves the organization toward a great workplace at a pace that is sustainable. Doing so involves learning from best practices while taking care to create practices that are unique and relevant to your organization. Moving at a sustainable pace also involves taking an approach to action planning that builds upon strengths while organically addressing areas of concern. But before you lead the charge, it is imperative that you begin with the right point of view.

THE PERSPECTIVE OF A GREAT LEADER

Even if you have a great culture, a whip-smart strategy, and undeniable presence in the market, you will still fall short of great company standards if you don't keep your focus on the *and*. Leaders who get it right execute on a strategy that takes into account the needs of their consumers *and* the needs of their employees. They recognize the importance of creating a product that both consumers *and* employees can feel good about. They realize that employees are key to creating a strategy that works *and* a customer experience that keeps them coming back.

We interviewed dozens of leaders for this book, many of whom have appeared throughout its chapters. On your behalf, we asked for advice. Specifically, we asked: What would you tell someone about your role as a leader? What is the importance of building trust? What have you learned from mistakes along the way? While we weren't surprised by leaders' answers, they inspired us. We also surmised yet another key leader imperative: great leaders are balanced in their approach to culture.

They see their role as a leader as an important one, but they don't falsely believe they can singlehandedly create or maintain a culture. And, while they take visible and decisive action, they also recognize that the fruits of their labors won't appear overnight.

While leaders in recognized companies are as different as you'd expect them to be, their comments on what it takes to create a great workplace reflect a balance of the tensions between responsibility and humility, between passion and patience, and between relationships and results. Great leaders don't choose one or the other; they balance both perspectives.

The First Balance: Responsibility and Humility

Many of the leaders we interviewed could define their job in their organizations' cultures clearly. They understand their important responsibility in creating and maintaining great workplaces, and rise to the challenges it brings. But they also know they can't do it alone. Great places to work have strong relationships, which means that *everyone* needs to be involved in building that great workplace. Great leaders make sure managers, supervisors, and employees understand their roles as well, and that the effort to build a great workplace is a group endeavor.

When describing her role in culture, Terri Kelly, CEO at W. L. Gore & Associates, says, "I feel fundamentally that making sure that the culture evolves in a healthy way—stewardship of the culture—is one of the most important roles that I play. It's very tricky. You've got to be able to adapt where you need to adapt to meet the business challenges, without losing the core of the company. So making a judgment about where we are on that line—of supporting the fundamental beliefs, but not getting behind and not having the culture hold you back—I don't think you can delegate that. You've got to have a very hands-on role. I put quite a bit of time into stewarding the culture, communicating the values, making sure our leaders live up to those values, and evolving our practices to make sure they meet today's challenges."

Keith Oden at Camden Property Trust also speaks about his personal commitment to creating a strong culture, "If you are committed to a great workplace, you can't kick it to HR or form some working group. You have to lead the charge. Now, it doesn't mean that you have to lift every bale and tote every barge, but you have to make the commitment and then enroll your senior executives. It has to be top-down in terms of commitment. Grassroots efforts are great, but for something like this, a change in a company's culture, you have to make a commitment, and it has to be a very visible commitment."

But great leaders balance their strong personal commitment with a humble belief that others have an important role as well. At Scripps Health, CEO Chris Van Gorder started the Scripps Leadership Academy as a powerful signal that responsibility needs to be shared. "I knew I had to change the culture, but I had been around long enough to realize *I* couldn't change the culture. It was the front-line manager and the front-line supervisor that would change the culture. So I created the Scripps Leadership Academy. And at the end of the program I said, 'I want you to be my agents of culture change. You understand how the system works now. I need you to call me when you have observations, when you think we are making mistakes. Call us on them, we can fix these things.'" Van Gorder has empowered dozens of managers and supervisors to change the culture, and they have. Scripps moved from a culture of widespread mistrust and competition to a list-making culture of pride and cohesion in 2008.

Rob Burton at Hoar Construction captures it this way. He says, "When it comes to specific issues, I think one of the biggest mistakes that CEOs make is to look forward to the power and the authority that they're given. My advice is, sure that's true, but take that and put it in your pocket because you don't need to use it. When you need to use it, it's there and everybody knows that. You can say no when you want to. The better thing to do is to forget about it and stay humble and go to work with your friends and get the job done. That's been my philosophy about it. It's not an ego trip. It's a lifestyle."

An example of the balance a leader strikes between responsibility and humility is that of Lisa Brummel. Brummel began her career as Corporate Vice President of Human Resources at Microsoft by listening to employees. Four months after she began her job, she reserved the largest conference room she could for her first town hall meeting. She laid out her take on employee concerns, and then opened the floor for employees to correct or support her analysis—a risky move for a new leader! But Brummel's perspective on her role sent her in a different direction. She says many leaders have a preconceived notion of what they want to accomplish, and they force that on people in the name of the leadership role. Her view is much different. She says, "You have to listen to people. You have to. People will tell you what's right and what's wrong. You have to be willing to get out there and hear what they have to say." Out of her conversations came My Microsoft, a way to package the employee experience. Like Microsoft software products, My Microsoft evolves and responds to employee needs just as a product responds to market needs. Brummel knows she can't create a successful product that doesn't meet the real needs of the customers, and she wasn't about to create My Microsoft without determining the real needs of the employees. It's one thing to tell employees a program is responsive to their needs and suggestions, and quite another thing to create the program while actively responding to their needs.

As a leader, you must accept responsibility for your role in culture. You are the chief role model and trust builder, and people look to your behavior and decisions for guidance on their own behavior and decision making. But you also need some degree of humility that allows you to reach out and enlist people. Your responsibility needs to become everyone's responsibility if you want to create a great workplace.

The Second Balance: Passion and Patience

Leaders at great workplaces put a priority upon people, not to the exclusion of strategy and marketplace, but as an important cornerstone of the organizations' success. They see the success of their companies as intimately tied to the health of their workplaces, and they want to take decisive action in order to make positive changes. They also know that building relationships takes time; it doesn't happen overnight.

No matter their role, leaders at great workplaces are passionate about how their work helps the companies to succeed. Though Vic Buzachero at Scripps Health rarely makes direct contact with a patient, he understands how he contributes. "My role is to really help to deliver outstanding patient care, and one tool is having an outstanding workforce and outstanding talent." While Buzachero's comment shows he *understands* how strategies and people are linked, Patrick O'Brien, President of Developed Markets at SC Johnson, talks about the importance of *communicating* that link. "Having a great place to work is a driver of key business results. It makes us a sustainable, strong concern for the long term. So, as I look back on my early mistakes, I could have done a better job at linking it—the more people are engaged, the more they're involved, the more they're going to be committed, the more we're going to get better results."

Balancing passion is patience. Great leaders are passionate about creating and maintaining a strong culture, but they know it doesn't happen quickly, and that it can take months or even years of activity before the culture shifts. Thomas Holder, CEO of Atlanta-based Holder Construction, says it this way, "I don't think it happens overnight. I think it's years and years of demonstrating your value system. I think if you have an organization that is not going so well, and you walk in and say, 'Okay, today we are going to have a strong value system, and this is going to be a great place to work'—forget that. You have to live it first. To get your people to buy into it, they have got to see you walk the walk, not only talk the talk, and they've got to believe it. The important thing for me is you have got to live it every day."

Bob Moritz, CEO of PricewaterhouseCoopers, illustrated the balance between passion and patience beautifully when he gave his advice on how to begin the process of creating a great workplace. "Spend the time. Don't rush to judgment. Think about what you want to become. Second, I think you need to take a realistic view of what you can accomplish and how it stacks against your other priorities. If you aren't willing to make it a top priority, it is never going to get on your personal agenda enough." Moritz makes it clear that your great workplace needs to be a top priority, but also advises thoughtfulness and realism in what you can accomplish. He goes on to say, "Then, I think you also need to figure out who are the right people who you will bank on to help drive it, the right leadership team. And then you have to think through what are the levers to pull to get the change you need. Is it programs? Maybe you need to put some programs in place. Compensation metrics? You've got to figure out what card to play and play it. The last thing is patience and persistence. It doesn't change overnight. Keep reminding yourself you are looking for incremental changes."

The Third Balance: People and Results
Leaders at great workplaces advise you to strike one last balance in your perspective: people and results. Here, we refer to the leader's people perspective as the keen understanding of the importance of people to the success of the enterprise. Behind every job description there is a person, and behind every organizational accomplishment there is a team of dedicated people. But while grateful for employees' contributions, leaders at great workplaces make their expectations for success clear and hold people accountable for results. Err on the people side, and your organization may be fun and caring, but not productive. Err on the results side, and goals are met, but people live in a state of burnout

and fear. As a leader, you need to be sure your managers understand this balance. You need to hold people accountable for great results, but also ensure that they are building a workgroup culture that values its people.

Mike Davis, SVP of Human Resources at General Mills, explained to us that their leaders are given regular feedback on their performance, and are required to attend to the people side of their operation. He told us, "Almost any time we take a leader out of their role, it's not because of performance, it's because he or she is failing fundamentally in the human side of what it is we're expecting him or her to do. When you think about it, when you put somebody in a role where they are responsible for other people, there is no more precious thing you can do. We take that pretty seriously. If you're in a people role, every three years at a minimum, you get feedback from those who work with you about how you're doing. Anybody who's in a managerial position goes through some level of centralized training. We owe people a minimum of a good, and hopefully great, boss."

At Camden, managers are held accountable because everyone in the organization is trained on what they should expect of their leaders. As Cindy Scharringhausen from Camden tells us, "Creating a great workplace is ultimately accomplished through total commitment. We see it from the top down and from the bottom up. People are judged on their ability to maintain our culture. You know as a manager what you are accountable for. When you train people on the front lines to know what the culture should be, they can tell us when their manager isn't doing it."

While some companies have feedback mechanisms and training that ensure this balance, Van Gorder at Scripps told us he personally shares the message with new managers. At Scripps, managers are held accountable to quality, safety, and financial metrics, but also to people metrics. He says, "I always teach at the new manager orientation that your biggest job in life is to take care of people. That is your job. If you take care of your people, they will take care of you. But I also talk about responsibility and accountability. I am pretty harsh on accountability. My definition of accountability is, you can miss your targets once. You won't be here to miss them twice. Pretty simple."

The point of view you have as a leader sets the tone for the entire organization. Your commitment to the organization's values is important, as is your passion about the role of people in your success. But these must be balanced with the belief that you can't create a culture on your own, and it's not going to happen overnight and without some degree of accountability. Once you've determined your own personal blend of responsibility, humility, passion, patience, people, and results, you can begin to put what you've learned into practice.

HOW TO MOVE FORWARD

At the outset of your journey, it is important to keep remembering that building a culture is less about what you do, and more about how you do it. In your next steps, continually strive to improve the *process* by which you communicate, train people, or pay people, for instance. The things you are already doing are obviously relevant to business success, so start by improving upon those things rather than assuming a great place to work comes from doing new and different things. Said another way, navigating your current operating environment (the how) is the key to culture, not creating something entirely new and different (the what). Consider best practices and then put them to work for *you*.

Using Best Practices

The best practices we've highlighted in this book are meant to inspire you to consider different ways trust, pride, and camaraderie might be built in your organization. We hope you feel inspired, but we also encourage you to remember two things about best practices: roots and relationships.

First, practices become part of the fabric of an organization because they are rooted in the values, history, industry, or operating environment of the company. Remember that culture arises when people successfully solve problems or capitalize upon opportunities in their environment, and success will be defined in the context of each company's values, history, industry, and operating environment. Consider how two organizations deal with gathering suggestions from their employees.

Given that Google is in the technology industry, uses and supports open source technology, and has a very collaborative work environment, it makes sense that their suggestion programs are online and open to everyone. As we discussed in Chapter 3, the "Google Ideas" website allows Googlers to regularly submit their thoughts on product improvements or suggestions about how to make things better around Google.

Google's practice wouldn't work as well at Scripps Health. At Scripps, many employees are on the move, and when they do have time in front of a computer, it isn't often for very long. Additionally, many people at Scripps came to the health care field in the first place because they value caring and concern. Face-to-face communication is a primary vehicle for gathering information. To this end, leaders engage in "rounding," which we discussed in Chapter 6. They stop by busy work environments to collect feedback, and to observe problems and opportunities as they occur. Additionally, SVP of Innovation, Human Resources and Performance Management Vic Buzachero conducts focus groups regularly to gather information directly from employees about key issues and areas for improvement.

This is not to say that a technological solution would never work at Scripps. In fact, their all-employee survey is taken online, and its organizers are proud of a near 100 percent response rate. Likewise, face-to-face meetings are important at Google. Remember that at times, the conversations started on "Google Ideas" become the topic of a larger discussion at a TGIF, Google's weekly company-wide get-together hosted by senior leaders. The important point is that leaders at both companies situate their solutions within the unique circumstances of their organizations, and create programs that are comfortable and intuitive to employees while capitalizing on an opportunity to build culture and drive results.

The second important thing to remember about best practices is that they become so when they strengthen the relationships that people have with the organization. The relationships themselves—trust, pride, and camaraderie—are relatively consistent across organizations. But the *people* in those relationships are different. People have unique skills and needs, and your people's skills and needs are likely different from those in an organization that may inspire you.

Bottom line? Because practices are in response to a unique set of circumstances and satisfy a unique set of employee needs, they can rarely be replicated completely with any degree of success. However, you can use them as a launch point for your journey. In order to incorporate the wisdom from best practices into your own organization, consider the following:

- What is the purpose of the practice? In other words, what problem does it solve or what opportunity does it help realize? How are these circumstances similar to or different from what we are facing?
- What resources do we have that would improve this practice's chances of succeeding? Sometimes these resources are tangible, like funds or equipment. Other times, they are intangible, like time or proximity. Think through what is already intact for the practice to be a success in your work environment.
- What challenges to implementing this practice would we face? Now, think about the tangible and intangible challenges to success. Is it possible to overcome these challenges in the immediate future? If not, perhaps this practice would need to be substantially modified in order to fit.

• Lastly, taking everything into account, what would the practice look like in our organization? Are there resources we can rely upon? Challenges we need to address first? Is there a different, more appropriate practice that would accomplish a similar degree of trust, pride, or camaraderie?

These questions are meant to help you determine what aspects of the practice might work for your organization, and what aspects may need to be altered or modified. Once you have a handle on the similarities and differences between each best practice and your unique set of circumstances, you are ready to use the wisdom from the best practices in action planning.

Action Planning

Action plans start with information. Creating a great workplace is no different. You need to understand the quality of relationships from the employee perspective. In our work, we gather information on trust, pride, and camaraderie from employees through surveys and focus groups. Regardless of how you collect that information, we suggest you use that information somewhat differently than you might have in the past.

One way you might use this information differently is to realize that any actions you take on the basis of the data are for the purpose of your workgroup's cultural development, not just your own, personal leadership development. Let's be clear on the distinction. In creating a personal action plan, you might determine how you will provide better feedback, or how you might do a better job at thanking people. When determining how to improve your workgroup's culture, you do those things, but you take it one step further. You need to take actions to build a workgroup *culture* where feedback is sought and readily shared. You need to create a *culture* of appreciation, where people recognize each other's strengths in both formal and informal ways. Your role modeling behaviors that you personally develop will go a long way, but you'll also need to enable others to behave differently to truly change a culture.

The other thing we suggest, which is somewhat counterintuitive, is to focus on your strengths as much as if not more than your opportunities. Most action planning guidelines, be they for personal or organizational development, suggest that you zero in on opportunity areas and create action steps that help you march those opportunity areas into areas of strength. While taking this approach might help you think of options and set deadlines for yourself, it's not the whole story. Great places to work grow from their strengths; they build upon what is already going well and the resources they already have at their disposal. It is human to zero in on all of the areas where you are not meeting the standards you've set for yourself, even the newly set standards you might now have for your organizational culture. We tend to focus upon the "C" in a report card full of "A's" without thinking about all of the great things that the "A's" allow us to do.

Once you identify your strengths and opportunities, think critically about their nature before proceeding. First, consider how your strengths can be used to help develop your opportunity areas. For example, say you think your workgroup needs some work in the encouragement of work-life balance. You can create an action plan to build a better sense of balance from scratch. But you might also consider what is going well that could help. For instance, you may have a strength in assigning and coordinating people. Perhaps you could build on that strength to create assignments that give more flexibility for your employees. Or perhaps your group's strength is a sense of community among people. If that is the case, perhaps they would respond best to encouragement and support from each other for a healthy work-life balance. Your strengths give you guidance as to the tactics that will be most successful in working on your areas of opportunity.

Second, often we find that opportunity areas are a function, at least in part, of the industry or the age of the organization. While hundreds of companies have been recognized on our lists over the years, we've never seen a perfect company. They all have strengths and areas of opportunity. While the best don't ignore their opportunity areas, they build them only to the level their operating environments will allow. And they focus doubly on building their strengths until they are bedrock to the culture, and part of their competitive advantage when it comes to talent.

Consider the example of Ernst & Young. Their busy season extends from January to April, tax season! While they will never be able to ease the stress of their employees during this time completely, they do all they can to make things easier, oftentimes using the strengths they have in other areas. For instance, Ernst & Young's family programs are extensive. They have adoption allowances and networking groups for parents of special needs children. And in addition to their regular backup care services, they offer a Saturday/Busy Season Child Care Program. The demands of the traditional "busy season" in their various practices require some people to work extra hours, often on weekends. This program enables parents to recoup the additional expense that the extra hours can cause. In this case, the opportunity area (stressful workloads during tax season) will be difficult if not impossible to ameliorate. But the area of strength in family assistance can be built upon despite this opportunity area, while in the process providing some relief to employees during this time.

Lastly, when you begin action planning in a particular area, you need to *think critically* about the strengths that you have in that area. You might be thinking you have no strengths at all if you've identified it as an opportunity area! But we've never encountered an organization where *nothing* was going well. Even if your strengths seem small, taking time to understand your own starting point helps you to take a measured next step, one that your leaders, peers, and employees are comfortable embracing. If you attempt to go too far too quickly, you will encounter resistance at best, and broken trust at worst. For example, you may wish that people felt comfortable using an open-door policy, or speaking up in meetings. But the best that people can do right now when it comes to suggestions is making comments on an anonymous survey. A reasonable next step may be to keep feedback anonymous, but to allow people to make suggestions any time of year. A step too far may be to allocate large amounts of time to an open forum discussion in a meeting. The anonymous suggestion system builds on what is going well while not pushing people out of their comfort zone.

Sometimes it is necessary to push people, but recognize that once you have a reservoir of trust built up, you will be met with less resistance. In the beginning stages of your journey, the need to take a reasonable next step rather than a huge leap is important. Successful change is like pulling a ripe apple off of a tree. Try to pull too soon, and not only is it more difficult to pick the apple, but it's sour once you bite into it.

Given these basic principles, we offer a simple guide to action planning using your best practices, the Great Place to Work Model, and your newly honed leadership point of view.

A Step-by-Step Guide

1. Choose Areas of Focus: An area of focus is a category or related group of categories where you will be placing the most attention over the next few months. Note that areas of focus are *not* action plans. They are areas that warrant your attention. You might have an inspirational best practice in each focus area, such as a sundown rule for responding to employee e-mails and phone calls if you want to focus on accessibility. Or, you might think about a signal of increased trust, pride, or camaraderie you'd like to work toward in that focus area. For instance, you may wish to become so accessible that people feel comfortable stopping by your office.

You should choose two to three areas of focus. While you may feel as though you want to work on more areas, there is a danger in spreading yourself too thin. It is better to make solid change in a few areas than unsustainable change in many areas. Moreover, you'll find that your results in other areas may improve as a byproduct of your focus in just two or three critical ones.

Try to get as close to the root cause of trust as possible. Remember that two-way communication underlies much of the Model. Chances are, if your two-way communication is an area of opportunity, any chances of building a greater sense of, say, impartiality are lower.

2. Take Inventory: Once you choose your areas of focus, determine two things. First, what strengths might help you with each area of focus? For example, if you hope to have a greater sense of hospitality for new hires, you might think about your own hiring practices. If you learn a lot about new hires in your interviews, you might use some of that information to customize their welcome. Alternatively, you may feel as though the sense of family in your workgroup is strong. How can you involve your employees in the welcoming process?

Second, take inventory of what is already going well in each area. This is your foundation for any action plans you create. You'll need to understand where you are starting from in order to behave in ways that build incremental trust without backfiring. For instance, in our example above, you might feel as though the first day an employee joins the company is a great experience; it is in the following days and weeks that the momentum drops. Understanding your starting point allows you to take appropriate next steps.

3. Map the Gap: The next step is to look at the gap between your inspirational best practice and your desired outcome, and to determine the first two to three steps that get you closer to where you *want* to be.

It may take several steps to get there, but beyond the first few, it is difficult to predict what might be most appropriate. We don't recommend building the entire plan for this reason. After you take the first few steps, you'll remap the gap. For instance, in our example above, a reasonable next step might be to ask your workgroup to arrange lunch plans for the remainder of the first week, or to plan a celebration on the person's one-month anniversary that is based upon his or her unique contributions to the team. The success (or failure) of these actions will tell you where to go next.

You'll also want to be realistic about the obstacles that may be in your work environment when it comes to working toward the best practice you've chosen. If you've answered the questions above about your chosen best practices, you should already have an idea of what these are. Remember that the gap may not be closed until you remove these obstacles. For instance, if there aren't funds to arrange for lunch for the entirety of the first week, you may need to plan for brown bag lunches. Or, if people in your workgroup are so rushed that a new hire's orientation falls through the cracks, you may want to assign a formal mentor or include the welcoming of new employees as part of your performance standards.

The first few steps are the most difficult, because they often feel slow and cumbersome. Like pushing a stalled car, it may take a great deal of effort to get things moving. But once there is some momentum, you should be able to move more quickly toward your desired practice or outcome, both because you've built more trust with your people and because you've become a better change champion.

4. Check Your Thinking: Before nailing down specific action steps in your areas of focus, have a conversation with people in your workgroup. You may want to share your analysis of strengths, resources, and opportunities to determine if you've been accurate in your approach. This type of conversation builds more trust, particularly in two-way communication, collaboration, and treating people as full members of your workgroup. Additionally, for many behavior shifts, you may need to rely upon members of your workgroup to either adjust to or support the shifts.

Every conversation is going to move along differently, and if you find yourself in a deficit situation when it comes to trust, you may want to attempt to make progress on some key behavior changes before sitting down with people. Or you may have private conversations as a first step. Below are some questions you may ask, using your own judgment as to how your group will respond:

- What is your general experience of our workgroup? What are some things you really appreciate? Are there other things you feel are obstacles to our being a great place to work? What am I doing, as a leader, when each of these things are happening?
- How do you feel about my focus on these two to three areas for the next few months? How does your behavior need to change if I take these steps? Would your experience be improved if we have success in these areas?
- Any ideas for how, specifically, I might make my action steps even more successful?

5. Take the First Step: You'd be surprised at how difficult this is sometimes! Managers have a tendency to want to wait until conditions are perfect before they act—until the rush dies down, until performance appraisal time is over, until they finish up their work on this year's budget. There is never a "wrong" time to deepen the trust relationship. If any of the conditions that stop you are present, think about how you can work within those to make progress, even if it means retooling your action plan. If things are rushed right now, how can new hires learn from that rush? If it is performance appraisal time, how might you show new hires their performance expectations even if they don't have a formal performance appraisal?

Even if managers take that first step, sometimes it is difficult to keep it up until a true change in the work environment is experienced. When managers make changes, even if they are for the better, it may take people time to adjust to the changes and respond appropriately. If you don't see immediate change, that's not a sign things aren't working. Trust builds over time, and you will need to ensure you have personal support from your leaders or mentors to help you continue to move forward even in the face of skepticism or confusion on the part of your employees.

6. Add to the Inventory and Remap the Gap: Once you've been successful at executing the first few steps in each area of focus, it is important to take inventory again and then remap the gap before generating action steps. We often find that progress in one area comes with additional benefits. In the process of taking action in one area, you may strengthen other areas, or build resources that can now be used to continue your journey. We recommend setting aside time to reflect at four- to six-month intervals as you take action to improve your workplace. As leaders at companies who have been recognized will tell you, this process never ends. There is always room to improve or modify your culture as the business environment, marketplace, and employee population change.

A great place to work won't materialize overnight, but it *will* come to be when people like you commit to making changes. You realize that your very success as an organization depends upon the health of your culture. People's workplace experience drives the experience of your customers and clients, and helps people to deliver on organizational strategies and goals.

We leave you with one last quote, from Danny Wegman of Wegmans Food Market. He now gives talks at business schools in the Northeast, and tries to impress upon people that business is a human enterprise.

He says, "That's what an organization is: a living, breathing organism, and it has to do with everyone around you and their values. When we wrote our values down they weren't aspirational values, they were real ones. We weren't writing down what we wanted to be, but what we believed in. That's how most of our people come to us—they visit our store and say, 'I like this. I'd like to be part of this,' and that's the really wonderful part about it, whether you are 14 or 80. And you ask, where did it come from? I think it's that we've always been committed to doing the right thing. And the more success you have at doing it, it just reinforces it."

Building a great place to work is building the relationships people have with their leaders, the relationships people have with their work, and the relationships people have with their coworkers. We wish for you and your employees more trust, pride, and camaraderie. We wish for you to always be a part of a great place to work.

REFERENCES AND RESOURCES

References

Edelman Trust Barometer 2010. Edelman Worldwide, 2010.

Edmans, A. *Does the Stock Market Fully Value Intangibles? Employee Satisfaction and Equity Prices*. Philadelphia: University of Pennsylvania, Wharton School, 2010.

Levering, R. L. *A Great Place to Work: What Makes Some Employers So Good—And Most So Bad*. New York: Random House, 1988.

Levering, R. L., & Moskowitz, M. *The 100 Best Companies to Work for in America*. Reading, MA: Addison Wesley, 1984.

Parella, T. *Fractured to Fortune*. Southlake, TX: Everythings Jake Publishing, 2008.

Ventrice, C. *Make Their Day! Employee Recognition That Works*. San Francisco: Berrett-Koehler, 2009.

Online Resources

Website for this book: http://www.thegreatworkplaceonline.com

Website for the Great Place to Work® Institute: http://www.greatplacetowork.com

Website for *The Great Workplace* training package (*A Great Place to Work: Building Trust and Driving Performance*): http://www.pfeiffer.com

Additional stories and best practices for which we didn't have room in the book: http://www.thegreatworkplaceonline.com/stories

Additional information on the business case: http://www.thegreatworkplaceonline.com/resources

Book recommendations and other useful links: http://www.thegreatworkplace online.com/links

Website of the authors: http://www.michaelburchell.com, http://www.jenniferrobin.net

Follow us on Twitter (@TheGreatWorkP): http://www.twitter.com

ACKNOWLEDGMENTS

First and foremost, we are indebted to the people at each organization that generously shared with us their time, their stories, and their insights. We interviewed leaders and employees at Camden Property Trust, CH2M HILL, General Mills, Google, W. L. Gore & Associates, Hoar Construction, Holder Construction, Microsoft, PricewaterhouseCoopers LLP, SAS, SC Johnson, Scripps Health, and Wegmans Food Markets. We left each interview with renewed delight that the world can be changed through great workplaces. These companies, and the scores of others cited in the book, are shining examples of what it means to do so.

While our names are on the cover, this book is the accomplishment of many people. There is a large team behind us, both at Jossey-Bass and the Great Place to Work Institute. Thank you to Genoveva Llosa, our editor, teacher, and friend. We've become better writers with every edit and come to appreciate you more with each conversation. Additional thanks to Jenna Land Free, whose congeniality and patience belied the tough love she gave our drafts. The manuscript became a book in Jenna's capable hands.

Many others at Jossey-Bass have also been nothing short of amazing. There's no way we'll be able to acknowledge all of them here, but we do want to thank Lisa Shannon, who blazed the trail; Gayle Mak and Susan Williams, who stepped in at a crucial time; Mark Karmendy, who helped us through the production process; and Carolyn Carlstroem, who has helped us to spread our message about great workplaces.

Our very special thanks to Robert Levering and Amy Lyman, founders of the Great Place to Work Institute. Your unwavering belief in a better society through great workplaces is an inspiration to leaders the world over. But both of you are also an inspiration to us. Your original thinking is the essence of this book, and we are grateful beyond measure for your unqualified belief in us to represent your ideas.

Words can't say enough about our esteemed colleagues at the Institute, in San Francisco and around the world, many of whom read drafts, answered questions, provided insights, and helped craft our message. Not only have each and every one of you helped us to become better leaders, we're proud to call you our friends. We are especially grateful to Ricardo Lange for sharing our vision, Leslie Caccamese for her marketing wizardry, Lisa Ratner for reaching out to our networks and friends, Sarah Lewis-Kulin for rallying our internal experts, Molly Webb and Nicole Petitti for helping us to make connections, and Palle Ellemann Knudsen and Otto Zell for providing their global perspective.

Michael would like to thank the Institute's global CEO, José Tolovi Jr., for giving me the space to focus on this project, and my colleagues on the corporate team who have been exceedingly patient with me as I juggled multiple responsibilities. Thank you to my parents, James and Carol Burchell, who taught me my first lessons in trust, and my brother, Daniel, who has been a constant support. David Robert took on additional work and supported me on a number of fronts, as did several other people, including Annie, Peter, Heather, Cheryl, Cathryn, and Warren. Thanks for your encouragement and for keeping me sane and healthy.

Jennifer would also like to thank my colleagues in the Foster College of Business for their support in writing this book. I am grateful to Larry Weinzimmer, who was always willing to read drafts and excerpts and provide his expert opinion. Thanks also to my personal board of directors, people who encourage me and keep me grounded—Stacy, Erin, Suzanne, Stephenie, Angela, Trish, Joy, Heidi, and many others. Your friendship is a gift. My appreciation also goes to Jenny Mandel, dog sitter extraordinaire. Last but not least, thank you to my family in Davenport. This book is as much your accomplishment as it is mine. Special thanks to my niece Matilda, who reminded me that I'm not just an author, but I am Auntie Bird and her favorite dance partner.

ABOUT THE AUTHORS

Michael Burchell, Ed.D., is Vice President for Global Business Development at the Great Place to Work Institute, Inc. A member of the corporate team, Michael oversees business development of multinational clients across the affiliate network, and supports affiliate growth and development worldwide. Previously, Michael led consulting services for the Institute in the U.S. He also co-owns the Great Place to Work Institute UAE based in Dubai.

Prior to joining the Institute, Michael worked at W. L. Gore & Associates and the University of Massachusetts. Michael received his doctorate from the University of Massachusetts Amherst, and also holds degrees from Colorado State University and the University of Southern California. Michael's address is in Washington, D.C., but he lives in seat 8A on flights to various destinations around the globe. You can find his website at www.michaelburchell.com.

Jennifer Robin, Ph.D., is a Research Fellow at the Great Place to Work Institute. A former consultant with the Institute, she led the Advisory

Practice, helping senior leaders integrate their organizations' cultures with their strategies and aligning efforts to be great workplaces. Currently, Jennifer teaches in undergraduate, MBA, and professional programs in the Foster College of Business at Bradley University. She serves as an adjunct consultant for the Institute and conducts research on the importance of values and stories to organizational culture and the leader behaviors that build trust.

Jennifer holds a Ph.D. in Industrial/Organizational Psychology from the University of Tennessee and undergraduate degrees in both Human Resource Management and Psychology from the University of Northern Iowa. She lives in Peoria, Illinois, with her dog Cooper. In her spare time, Jennifer can be found on hiking trails, in airports, or writing in coffee shops. Her website can be found at www.jenniferrobin.net.

The Great Place to Work Institute is a global assessment and advisory firm, based in San Francisco, California, with affiliate offices in over 40 countries. Co-founded by best-selling business author Robert Levering and organizational consultant Amy Lyman, Ph.D., in collaboration with a team of professionals committed to the recognition and development of great workplaces around the world, the Institute's mission is to build a better society by helping companies transform their workplaces. The Institute does this by helping companies improve corporate performance and raise the quality of work life for employees.

The Great Place to Work Institute works with FORTUNE magazine, *The Economic Times, The Financial Times,* and other leading publications in various countries to publish and recognize the Best Companies to Work For. They also provide advisory and assessment services for organizations, offer annual conferences on creating trust in the workplace, and continually research best practices at companies everywhere. You can find the Institute's website at www.greatplacetowork.com.

INDEX

A

Abbenhuijs, Frank, 188

Accenture, 170–171

Accessible communications, 34–38

Action plans, 214–221; choosing focus of, 217–218; consulting others about, 219–220; critical thinking required for, 216–217; focusing on strengths, 215, 216, 218; inventories for, 218; mapping gaps in, 218–219; reinventory and remap, 221; taking steps in, 220–221

ACUITY, 6

Adobe, 37

Aflac, 156–157, 168

Agilent, 132

Alston & Bird, 32

American Arbitration Association (AAA), 116

American Express, 114–115, 117–118

American Fidelity Assurance, 102–103

Analytical Graphics, 145–146

Appeals, 114–116

Arnold & Porter LLP, 144

B

Bain & Company, 141–142

Baird, Robert W., 75, 99

Baptist Health Care, 74

Becton Dickinson Canada Inc., 198

Benefits: expressing corporate respect with, 83–84; offering company health care, 81; SAS,

Corporations. *See* Corporate
culture; Companies; Global
corporations
Creativity: balancing global
consistency with local,
200; employing in benefits
programs, 25
Credibility, 27–60; about,
8; applying principles in
Netherlands, 197–198;
checklist for, 51–52; ensuring
establishment of, 49–50;
establishing competence,
38–44; evaluating leaders',
28; in Great Place to Work
Model, 4; integrity and, 44–48;
persisting in demonstration
of, 48–49; placing function
before form, 48; predictability
supporting, 51; trust and,
27–29, 49; two-way
communication and, 29–30, 50,
51–52; upholding corporate, 9
Culture Audits, 5–6
Customer service, 151
CXtec, 164–165

D
Davis, Mike, 89–90, 210
Davis, Ray, 50
Decision making: employee-made

compensation decisions,
102–103; engaging employees
in, 64; fairness in, 98–99;
impartiality in, 107–110;
transparency in, 98; W.L. Gore
& Associates principles for,
75–76
Deloitte, 163
Departure memos, 160–161
DePeters, Jack, 84, 151
Diversity: corporate support
for, 112, 113; encouraging
employee's, 97; fostering
culture of inclusion, 110–111;
global corporations addressing,
193–196
DreamWorks Animation, 78

E
EBay, 37, 45–46, 135
Edelman Trust Barometer, 17
Edmans, Alex, 13
Edward Jones, 36, 41
Efficiency and employee
satisfaction, 14
Eileen Fisher, 74
Employees: allowing boundary-
less organizations, 146;
appealing unfair decisions,
114–116; appreciating
perspective of, 86; asking

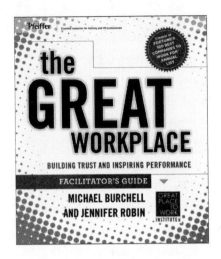

THE GREAT WORKPLACE:

Building Trust and Inspiring Performance Facilitator's Guide Set

Michael Burchell | Jennifer Robin

ISBN: 978-0-470-59835-1/2| US $225.00 | CAN $270.00

The Great Workplace lays out ideas that can help turn any workplace into a great one. At Zappos .com, we take these ideas seriously. Our company culture is our #1 priority. —**Tony Hsieh, CEO, Zappos.com, Inc. and #1 *New York Times* bestselling author, *Delivering Happiness***

The Great Workplace: Building Trust and Inspiring Performance Facilitator's Guide Set is a training package and assessment tool that introduces the concept and model behind A Great Place to Work (where employees trust the people they work for, have pride in what they do, and enjoy the people they work with), developed in 1984 and validated through its enduring resonance in both the United States and in 40 countries around the world. This training package provides strategies and development activities for applying the model in the workplace.

Great Place to Work® Institute has been conducting research on the characteristics of great workplaces for more than 25 years. Their research shows that leaders and managers in great workplaces strive to create a culture of trust in the workplace, fostering an environment in which employees take pride in what they do and enjoy the people they do it with. The model they have developed reflects these key relationships and further defines how it all plays out in the Five Dimensions of a Great Place to Work: Credibility, Respect, Fairness, Pride, and Camaraderie.

Learn more at www.pfeiffer.com/go/greatworkplace

An Imprint of ⊕WILEY

Now you know.